Messianic Prophecies

by

Greg Litmer

ISBN 10: 1-58427-300-3

ISBN 13: 978-158427-300-4

Guardian of Truth Foundation
P.O. Box 9670
Bowling Green, Kentucky 42102
1-800-428-0121
www.truthbooks.net

Table of Contents

Introduction

In John 5:39-40 Jesus was speaking to certain leaders of the Jews, and He told them, "You search the Scriptures, because you think that in them you have eternal life; it is these that testify about Me; and you are unwilling to come to Me, that you may have life."

This will be the goal of our study – we will seek to search the Scriptures to find their witness concerning the Lord Jesus Christ, because it is only in Him and through Him that we can find eternal life. When Jesus made the aforementioned statement, He was referring to the Old Testament scriptures, for they are alive with specific prophecies and a host of references concerning Him Who was to come – Jesus the Messiah.

This will be a study of Messianic Prophecy. It will not be exhaustive, for it is conservatively estimated that there are over 300 references to the Christ in the Old Testament, all of which are fulfilled in Jesus. We will focus our attention on fifty-six major prophecies. However, several others will be mentioned as our study progresses.

As is the case with any profitable study, a foundation must be laid and a method of approach determined. This we will do by defining certain pertinent terms, showing the importance placed upon prophecy by Jesus and His apostles, and by answering a potentially difficult question concerning our exegesis before it arises. With these introductory remarks, let us begin by defining terms important to the study.

Definition of Terms

Messiah – "A Hebrew word, to which the Greek word, *Christos*, answers. It was applicable to any person anointed with the holy oil: as the high priest (Lev. 4:3, 5, 16; 1 Sam. 12:3, 5; Hebrew) or the king (2 Sam. 1:14, 16). The title is given to the patriarchs, Abraham and Isaac, and to the Persian king, Cyrus, as chosen ones to administer the kingdom of God (Psa. 105:15; Isa. 45:1). When God promised David that the throne and scepter should remain in his family forever (2 Sam. 7:13), the title acquired a special reference and denoted the representative of the royal line of David (Pss. 2:2; 18:50; 84:9; 89:38, 51: 132:10, 17; Lam. 4:20; Hab. 3:13). And when prophecy began to tell of a king who should appear in this line and be the great deliverer of his people (Jer. 23:5-6), whose goings forth are from of old, from everlasting (Mic. 5:2-5), and who should uphold the throne and kingdom of David forever (Isa. 9:6-7), the title of the Messiah, par excellence, naturally became attached to him (Dan. 9:25-26), and ultimately became a customary designation of him, being as common as the title Son of David (John 1:41; 4:25) and in the form Christ (Matt. 1:1)" (*Davis Dictionary of the Bible*, 518).

It is interesting that three times this title, in its Greek form, was expressly applied to Jesus and accepted by Him (Matt. 16:17; Mark 14:61-62; John 4:26).

2. *Prophet* – "According to the uniform teaching of the Bible the prophet is a speaker of or for God. His words are not the production of his own spirit, but come from a higher source. For he is at the same time, also, a seer, who sees things that do not lie in the domain of natural sight or who hears things which human ears do not ordinarily receive" (*The International Standard Bible Encyclopedia*, IV: 2459).

"The prophet was one upon whom the Spirit of God rested (Num. 11:17-29); one to whom and through whom God speaks (Num. 12:2; Amos 3:7)" (Vine's *Expository Dictionary of New Testament Words*).

3. *Prophecy* – "Signifies the speaking forth of the mind and counsel of God . . . though much of Old Testament prophecy was purely

predictive, as Micah 5:2, e.g., and cp. John 11:51. Prophecy is not necessarily, nor even primarily, foretelling. It is the declaration of that which cannot be known by natural means (Matt. 26:68). It is the forth-telling of the will of God, whether with reference to the past, the present, or the future" (Vine's *Expository Dictionary of New Testament Words*).

4. *Fulfillment* – "In genuine prophecy, according to biblical conceptions, the fulfillment constituted an integral part. This is set up by Deuteronomy 18:21f as a proof of the genuineness of a prophetic utterance. The prophetic word 'falls to the ground' (Isa. 3:19) if it is not raised up (fulfilled) by the course of events . . . the fulfillment can be judged by the contemporaries in the sense of Deuteronomy 18:22 only when this fulfillment refers to the near future and when special emphasis is laid on external events. In these cases it is only later generations who can judge of the correctness of a prediction or a threat. . . . It is therefore not correct to demand a fulfillment pedantically exact with the form of the historical garb of the prophecy. The main thing is that the Divine thought contained in the prophecy be entirely and completely realized. This is especially the case in the New Testament in the appearance of the Son of Man, in whom all the rays of Old Testament prophecy have found their common center" (*The International Standard Bible Encyclopedia*, IV).

5. *Messianic Prophecy* – In this work this term will be used to refer to all prophecy that concerns the person, work, or kingdom of Jesus the Christ. This will be so whether there is express mention of the Christ or not.

The Importance of Messianic Prophecy

The significance of the Messianic Prophesy contained in the Old Testament and fulfilled in the person and work of the Lord Jesus cannot be over-emphasized. It is generally believed that the last book of the Old Testament, Malachi, was completed between 445–400 B.C. Should an individual refuse to accept that the Old Testament was completed at least 400 years before the birth of Jesus, they would still find themselves facing another very important fact. During the reign of Ptolemy Philadelphus, son of Ptolemy I who was one of Alexander the Great's prominent generals and who seized the satrapy of Egypt after Alexander's death, a Greek translation of the Hebrew scriptures was completed. It is known as the *Septuagint* and has to be dated somewhere between 285-246 B.C., the years of Ptolemy Philadelphus' reign. This means that, at the very least, the prophecies that were fulfilled in Jesus, of which there are hundreds, had been written and existed 250 years before they began to be fulfilled. When the Dead Sea Scrolls were found, included among them were a copy of the book of Isaiah and fragments of other books that are dated over a hundreds before Jesus' birth. This truth alone completely rules out any idea of intentional or coincidental fulfillment. The man or woman who refuses to recognize this is simply not being honest in his or her approach to the Scriptures or to the Lord.

Another extremely important aspect of Messianic Prophecy is the fact that Jesus Himself repeatedly appealed to it as proof that He was the Messiah. He called upon the people to examine the Old Testament prophecies concerning the One who was to come and to recognize what they were seeing, that those very prophecies were being fulfilled in Jesus. We have already noticed the Lord's statement in John 5:39, "You search the Scriptures, because you think that in them you have eternal life; it is these that testify about Me."

Let's notice a few others:

> And He came to Nazareth, where He had been brought up; and as was His custom, He entered the synagogue on the Sabbath, and stood up to read. And the book of the prophet Isaiah was handed to Him. And He opened the book and found the place where it was written, "The Spirit of the Lord is upon Me, because He anointed Me to preach the gospel to the poor. He has sent Me to proclaim release to the captives, and recovery of sight to the blind, to set free those who are oppressed, to proclaim the favorable year of the Lord." And He closed the book, gave it back to the attendant, and sat down; and the eyes of all in the synagogue were fixed on Him. And He began to say to them, "Today this Scripture has been fulfilled in your hearing" (Luke 4:16-21).

Now He said to them, "These are My words which I spoke to you while I was still with you, that all things which are written about Me in the Law of Moses and the Prophets and the Psalms must be fulfilled" (Luke 24:44).

At that time Jesus said to the crowds, "Have you come out with swords and clubs to arrest Me as you would against a robber? Every day I used to sit in the temple teaching and you did not seize Me. But all this has taken place to fulfill the Scriptures of the prophets" (Matt. 26:55-56a).

As the remainder of the New Testament was being written, we find the Apostles and other inspired writers making frequent references to the Messianic prophecies as having been fulfilled in Christ and presenting them as proof that Jesus was the Promised One. Let's notice some of these references beginning with the book of Acts:

You know of Jesus of Nazareth, how God anointed Him with the Holy Spirit and with power, and how He went about doing good, and healing all who were oppressed by the devil, for God was with Him. We are witnesses of all the things He did both in the land of the Jews and in Jerusalem. They also put Him to death by hanging Him on a cross. God raised Him up on the third day and granted that He become visible, not to all the people, but to witnesses who were chosen beforehand by God, that is, to us who ate and drank with Him after He arose from the dead. And He ordered us to preach to the people, and solemnly to testify that this is the One who has been appointed by God as Judge of the living and the dead. Of Him all the prophets bear witness that through His name everyone who believes in Him receives forgiveness of sins (Acts 10:38-43).

And according to Paul's custom, he went to them, and for three Sabbaths reasoned with them from the Scriptures, explaining and giving evidence that the Christ had to suffer and rise again from the dead, and saying, "This Jesus whom I am proclaiming to you is the Christ" (Acts 17:2-3).

Paul, a bond-servant of Christ Jesus, called as an apostle, set apart for the gospel of God, which He promised beforehand through His prophets in the holy Scriptures, concerning His Son, who was born of a descendant of David according to the flesh (Rom.

You also, as living stones, are being built up as a spiritual house for a holy priesthood, to offer up spiritual sacrifices acceptable to God through Jesus Christ. For this is contained in Scripture: "Behold I lay in Zion a choice stone, a precious corner stone, and he who believes in Him will not be disappointed." This precious value, then, is for you who believe. But for those who disbelieve, "The stone which the builders rejected, this became the very corner stone," and, "A stone of stumbling and a rock of offense"; for they stumble because they are disobedient to the word, and to this doom they were also appointed (1 Pet. 2:5-8).

Josh McDowell, in his book *Evidence that Demands a Verdict*, lists the following points of significance concerning Messianic Prophecy:

1c. Concludes that there is a divine intellect behind the Old and New Testaments
2c. Establishes the fact of God
3c. Authenticates the deity of Jesus
4c. Evinces the inspiration of the Bible

A study of Messianic Prophecy serves to increase the faith of a Christian in God the Father, in the inspiration of the Scriptures, and in the fact that Jesus is the Christ, the Son of the living God. For the open-hearted individual who has not yet become a follower of the Lord, it is my prayer that this brief examination of such a massive and wondrous subject will convince you to obey the Lord and serve Him faithfully all the remaining days of your life.

A Question of Approach

As we begin to examine the prophecies, there is a question which must first be answered. It will help to clarify the approach I will be taking. The question is: Is it possible for prophetic statements now recognized as Messianic to have had both an immediate or contemporary fulfillment for those to whom they were originally spoken and an ultimate fulfillment in Christ?

The answer is a qualified "yes." By way of illustration consider just one prophecy, Numbers 24:17: "I see him, but not now; I behold him, but not near; a star shall come forth from Jacob, a scepter shall rise from Israel, and shall crush through the forehead of Moab, and tear down all the sons of Sheth." Concerning this passage E.W. Hengstenberg noted in *Christology of the Old Testament*:

> By this Ruler, the Jews from the earliest times have understood the Messiah, either exclusively, or else, principally, with a secondary reference to David. Either its exclusive relation to the Messiah was maintained, or it was allowed to refer indeed, in the first instance, to David; but then both himself and his temporal victories were regarded as typical of Christ, and His spiritual triumphs, which the prophet had especially in view.

For further explanation consider this rather lengthy statement from *The International Standard Bible Encyclopedia*:

> The ideal of the Hebrew prophets and poets is amply fulfilled in the person, teaching, and work of Jesus of Nazareth. Apologists may often err in supporting the argument from prophecy by an extravagant symbolism and a false exegesis: but they are right in the contention that the essential elements of the Old Testament conception–the Messianic king who stands in a unique relation to Jehovah as His "Son," and who will exercise universal dominion; the supreme prophet who will never be superceded; the priest forever–are gathered up and transformed by Jesus in a way the ancient seers never dreamed of. As the last and the greatest prophet, the suffering Son of Man, and the sinless Savior of the world, He meets humanity's deepest longings for Divine knowledge, human sympathy and spiritual deliverance; as the unique Son of God who came to reveal the Father, He rules over the hearts of men by the might of eternal love. No wonder that the New Testament writers, like Jesus Himself, saw references to the Messiah in Old Testament passages which would not be conceded by a historical interpretation. While recognizing the place of the old covenant in the history of salvation, they sought to discover in the light of the fulfillment in Jesus the meaning of the Old Testament which the Spirit of God intended to convey, the Divine, saving thoughts which constitute its essence. And to us, as to the early Christians "the testimony of Jesus is the spirit of prophecy" (Revelation 19:10). To Him, hidden in the bosom of the ages, all the scattered rays of prophecy pointed: and from Him, in His revealed and risen splendor, shine forth upon the world the light and power of God's love and truth.

And through the history and experience of His people He is bringing to larger realization the glory and passion of Israel's Messianic hope (III, 2043-2044).

This will be the direction that this work will take. We will seek to determine first and foremost the meaning in the prophecies "which the Spirit of God intended to convey." A primary purpose of prophecy was to prepare the way for Jesus so that, when He came, He would be readily identifiable by a comparison to those prophecies that spoke of Him. To this end an amazingly in-depth picture was painted in the Old Testament of the Promised One. But we must remember that this picture was not presented to the Jews in its totality all at once. It was a gradual process. Through the centuries as various events transpired in the history of the Hebrew nation, the Holy Spirit revealed more and more of the picture as the people were able to understand it. Hengstenburg makes an interesting observation about this gradual process:

> The Messiah, therefore, could not be fully exhibited, until history had given to the Prophets materials from which their metaphorical representatives could be formed. The earlier theocracy supplied no sufficient groundwork for a complete delineation of Him. His character and offices, therefore, first appear fully unfolded in the time of David, to whom the Messiah was promised as a descendant. As the visible theocracy then furnished the materials for the representation of the Messiah's kingdom, so the typical head of the former served as the model of all that should be said for the glory of his antitype, the head of the latter (*Christology of the Old Testament*, 12).

This study will not be concerned with examining the prophecies in the chronological order in which they were given. While some attention will be paid to the extent of understanding that those to whom the prophecies were originally uttered had, our concern will be how the New Testament presents their ultimate fulfillment. The emphasis concerning the prophecies will be as they pertain to Jesus. As John wrote in Revelation 19:10, "The testimony of Jesus is the spirit of prophecy."

Chapter One

Prophecies Concerning Pre-existence

Micah 5:2, Isaiah 9:6

But as for you, Bethlehem Ephrathah, too little to be among the clans of Judah, from you One will go forth for Me to be ruler in Israel. His goings forth are from long ago, from the days of eternity (Mic. 5:2).

For a child will be born to us, a son will be given to us; and the government will rest on His shoulders; and His name will be called Wonderful Counselor, Mighty God, Eternal Father, Prince of Peace (Isa. 9:6).

Both of these passages indicate something that would be extraordinarily unique about the Ruler who was to come. Unlike temporal rulers and kings whose very lives are limited and bound by time, their reigns even more so, the promised Ruler would have no such boundaries or limitations. His rule reaches back into eternity.

Note a few comments concerning the statement in Micah 5:2: "His goings forth are from long ago, from the days of eternity."

From Jamieson, Fausett, & Brown's *Commentary on the Whole Bible*: "The plain antithesis of this clause, 'to come forth out of thee' (from Bethlehem), shows that the eternal generation of the Son is meant. The terms convey the strongest assertion of infinite duration of which the Hebrew language is capable" (817).

From Matthew Henry's *Commentary in One Volume*: "It is he

that is to be ruler in Israel, whose goings forth have been from of old, from everlasting, from the days of eternity, as the word is. This description of Christ's eternal generation, or his going forth as the Son of God, begotten of his Father before all worlds, shows that this prophecy must belong only to him, and could never be verified of any other" (1153).

From Homer Hailey, in *A Commentary on the Minor Prophets*, "indicates more than that He descends from an ancient lineage; it relates Him to God, the eternal One. His rule reaches back into eternity" (209).

In Isaiah 9:6, the same attribute is being applied to the Ruler who was to come with the title, "Eternal Father," or literally, "The Father of eternity." Hengstenberg's comments about this title fairly well summarize the thoughts of many of the scholars that I referenced, so from *Christology of the Old Testament*, the following is presented:

> Either we may suppose, that Father of eternity is the same as Eternal Father, when the meaning would be, that the Messiah will not, as must be the case with an earthly king, however excellent, leave his people destitute after a short reign, but rule over them, and bless them for ever. Or we may explain it by the usage of the Arabic, in which he who possesses a thing, is called the father of it, e.g. the father of mercy, the merciful . . . Father of eternity is the same as eternal. According to both explanations, the latter of which is much to be preferred, a Divine attribute is here ascribed to the Messiah (179-180).

Fulfillment – Colossians 1:17 & John 1:1-2

He is before all things, and in Him all things hold together (Col. 1:17).

In the beginning was the Word, and the Word was with God, and the Word was God. He was in the beginning with God (John 1:1-2).

A fundamental teaching of the New Testament is the eternal existence of our Lord and Savior Jesus Christ. As promised by the prophets, He who was to come would be eternal, and as pointed out by the passages above, the ultimate fulfillment of those promises was found in Christ.

Concerning Colossians 1:17, Albert Barnes, in *Barnes' Notes on the New Testament*, wrote, "The fair and proper meaning of the word 'before' is that he was before all things in the order of existence. It is equivalent to saying that he was eternal – for he that had an existence before anything was created must be eternal."

About no other individual can such a statement as Colossians 1:17 be made. Truly, no other individual in the history of mankind fulfills the unique qualification set forth in Micah and Isaiah – eternal existence. Jesus is the pre-existent Ruler who was promised.

When we discuss the life of Christ we must go back before the beginning. Now one could ask, "What beginning?" The answer would be the beginning of creation, the beginning of time. John starts his gospel with the same words Moses used to begin the book of Genesis, "In the beginning." John asserts that "in the beginning" the Word already was. The essential elements of time are a beginning and an ending. Since the Word (later identified as Jesus in John 1:14) already existed at the beginning of time, it is an inescapable conclusion that the Word must have been timeless – no beginning and no end. The Word existed at the beginning of creation and therefore was not created. The Word, Jesus, is eternal.

Chapter Two

Prophecies Concerning His Birth

In this chapter we will be turning our attention to nine prophecies concerning the birth of the Messiah. Many of the prophecies can be found more than once in the pages of the Old Testament, but we will not be examining each instance where similar prophecies occur. We will examine one Old Testament passage where the prophecy is found and appropriate New Testament passages that demonstrate its fulfillment. Even as we limit our study in this way, an honest seeker of truth cannot help but to be impressed by the exactness of some of the details found in the prophecies. They are of such a nature as to leave no doubt concerning their fulfillment. Only one individual meets the specifics set forth in every case – Jesus the Lord.

As I write these words in preparation for embarking on the examination of the prophecies concerning the birth of our Lord, I find myself thinking about a couple of objections that have been presented to me in the past by those who were skeptical. The objections can be simply stated. They are that the fulfillment of prophecy by Jesus was either intentional or coincidental. I believe that an open investigation of these nine prophecies answers both of those objections. Even the most skeptical must admit that it would be extremely difficult for one not yet born to intentionally fulfill anything. One of the prophecies refers to one who was to be born before Jesus; several others refer to the Lord's mother. Still others refer to events that happened while Jesus was a babe in the arms of Mary. Even the most hardened and determined unbeliever must admit that intentional fulfillment is not a valid objection to be raised regarding prophecies concerning our Lord's birth.

But what of coincidence? Let's draw a parallel. I have a son who was born in 1978. Now let us suppose that at least 250 years prior to that time (I use 250 years to accommodate the skeptics who must admit that the prophecies existed at least that long before they were fulfilled due to the existence of the Septuagint), in approximately the year 1728, five different men wrote about his birth. None of these men knew each other and none had a complete understanding of all the aspects of what they were writing about.

- One writes that a child will be born in Jewish Hospital in Cincinnati, Ohio.

- Another writes that this child will be born to a woman named Vicky Denise Litmer who has brown hair.

- Still another writes that the labor will last for two days and the birth will finally be a caesarean delivery performed by a Jewish doctor named Youkilis.

- Yet another writes that two people named Russ and Yvonna will come bearing gifts.

- Finally, the other writes that the child, to be named Adam, will reside in Reading, Ohio for two years and then move to Hillsboro, Ohio.

Ridiculous, some might say. Yet the prophecies concerning the birth of Jesus are that detailed, that exact. Coincidence does not enter into the picture.

1. Born of the Seed of Woman and the Initial Promise – Genesis 3:15

And I will put enmity between you and the woman, and between your seed and her seed; he shall bruise you on the head, and you shall bruise him on the heel (Gen. 3:15)

I have chosen to include Genesis 3:15 in this chapter because it bears directly on the nature of Christ's birth and is the initial promise of One who was to come. Adam and Eve had sinned, and spiritual and physical death had entered into the world. They were to leave the Garden of Eden, lose access to the Tree of Life, the serpent was cursed, the ground was cursed and woman was placed under subjection to man. Yet there is a ray of hope.

"God remembers mercy, and the first great promise of the coming Savior is given in verse 15" (J. Sidlow Baxter, *Explore the Book*, 39).

Genesis 3:15, known as the *Protoevangelium*, is the initial promise of a coming Savior, a coming Deliverer. Contained in the prophecy are three things of great importance pertaining to Jesus: (1) He was to be of the seed of woman. What makes this so interesting is that additional prophecies make it clear that He was to be born of the seed of woman only – meaning He was to be born of a virgin and not according to the natural process; (2) His suffering and death, while not precisely outlined, are certainly implied with the phrase "you shall bruise him on the heel"; (3) We also see an indication of the ultimate victory that would be won by He who was to come. Yes, Satan would "bruise him on the heel," but He would "bruise" the head of Satan. A wound to the heel, while painful, is not fatal. A blow to the head can kill. This destructive blow was accomplished when the Lord rose from the dead.

Let's notice a few comments about this passage from other writers.

Homer Hailey, *From Creation to the Day of Eternity*:

In pronouncing this curse God was not speaking of the snake family, but of the enmity that should exist between Satan, who is called "that old serpent" (Revelation 12:9), and man, the offspring of God (Acts 17:29). The promise was that "the seed of the woman" should bruise the devil's head. This promise, made at least four thousand years before its fulfillment, was the first indication that one should be born of woman apart from the natural begettal by the man.

In bruising the serpent's head this "seed of the woman" would have his heel bruised in the conflict. The head represents power. Though the serpent would not be completely destroyed, his power would be broken; he would be badly bruised until ultimately this blow would result in his destruction (Revelation 20:10). In accomplishing this, the "seed of woman" should have his heel bruised. This is a figurative expression suggesting a comparison between the blow rendered and the cost to accomplish it; Satan's power was broken through the death of Jesus Christ (31-32)

David L. Cooper wrote in *God and Messiah*:

In Genesis 3:15 we find the first prediction relative to the Savior of the world, called "the seed of the woman." In the original oracle God foretold the age-long conflict which would be waged between "the seed of the woman" and "the seed of the serpent"; and which will eventually be won by the former. This primitive promise indicates a struggle between the Messiah of Israel, the Savior of the world, on one hand, and Satan, the adversary of the human soul, on the other. It foretells complete victory eventually for the Messiah."

Fulfillment – Matthew 1:20-25

But when he had considered this, behold, an angel of the Lord appeared to him in a dream, saying, "Joseph, son of David, do not be afraid to take Mary as your wife; for the Child who has been conceived in her is of the Holy Spirit. She will bear a Son; and you shall call His name Jesus, for He will save His people from their sins." Now all this took place to fulfill what was spoken by the Lord through the prophet: "Behold, the virgin shall be with child and shall bear a Son, and they shall call His name 'Immanuel,' which translated means, 'God with us.'" And Joseph awoke from his sleep and did as the angel of the Lord commanded him, and took Mary as his wife, but kept her a virgin until she gave birth to a Son; and he called His name Jesus (Matt. 1:20-25).

While considering his course of action, Joseph was visited by the angel of the Lord in a dream. He received assurance that corroborated what Mary had apparently told him. The child she was carrying was of the Holy Spirit. He would be called Jesus; that is, Savior (being derived from the verb signifying "to save"). The promise had been that one would come of "the seed of woman." He is the only individual who met the requirement of being born of "the seed of woman" only.

The point should be made that many believe that Matthew gives the genealogy of Joseph, thus making Jesus his "legal" son and "legally" of the line of David. These same individuals believe that Luke gives the genealogy of Mary, making the Lord the biological son of Mary and naturally of the line of David as well.

2. Born of a Virgin – Isaiah 7:14

Therefore the Lord Himself will give you a sign: Behold, a virgin will be with child and bear a son, and she will call His name Immanuel (Isa. 7:14).

Isaiah 7:14 has proven to be one of the more controversial Messianic prophecies. It has proven to be so because many simply refuse to accept the idea of a virgin birth and choose to reject a plain statement made by Matthew concerning the fulfillment of this prophecy. The prophecy was uttered during the time of Ahaz, king of Judah. At that time Israel and Syria joined forces to overthrow the southern kingdom over which Ahaz ruled. King Ahaz was frightened and in despair. To Ahaz, Jehovah sent Isaiah and his son, Shearjashub, to assure the king that his enemies would not prevail. To corroborate the prophecy, Isaiah told Ahaz to ask the Lord for a sign, a miracle, either "deep as Sheol or high as heaven" (Isa. 7:11). Ahaz refused and Isaiah uttered the prophecy to the "house of David" (Isa. 7:13). A virgin would conceive and bear a son.

Much attention has been paid to the Hebrew word translated "virgin" in Isaiah 7:14. Many contend that "virgin" is an incorrect translation, that it should be rendered "young woman." The word itself is *almah*. Actually, of the two words rendered "virgin" in the Old Testament, *bethulah* and *almah*, *almah* is the one always used of a virgin.

William F. Beck wrote, "I have searched exhaustively for instances in which *almah* might mean a non-virgin or a married woman. There is no passage where *almah* is not a virgin. Nowhere in the Bible or elsewhere does *almah* mean anything but a virgin" ("What Does *Almah* Mean?" *The Lutheran News*, April 3, 1967).

Guy N. Woods writes, "The word occurs in the following instances and in each obviously designates an unmarried woman and a true virgin – Psa. 68:15, Ex. 2:8, Prov. 30:19, Gen. 24:43, Song of Solomon 1:3, 6:8, and Isa. 7:14" (*The Living Messages of the Books of the Old Testament*, 261).

Concerning Isaiah 7:14, Hengstenberg wrote:

Ahaz had refused the proffered sign, and the Prophet was compelled to relinquish the hope of raising him to confidence in Jehovah. But he must have been desirous that the deliverance should not be regarded, when it came, as the work of chance, but ascribed to the mercy of the Supreme Ruler of the theocracy: and that the confidence of the pious in Him should be confirmed. He therefore gives a sign, even against the will of Ahaz, whereby the confidence of every true member of the theocracy, in the prediction already given concerning the deliverance from the confederated kings, must be strengthened. I behold, he declares, the wonderful event of futurity, the birth of a Divine Redeemer of a virgin (*Christology of the Old Testament*, 152).

To put it simply, Isaiah 7:14 prophesied of the virgin birth of the coming Messiah. This child would be called "Immanuel," meaning "God with us." This brings to mind the words of John in John 1:14, "And the Word became flesh, and dwelt among us, and we beheld His glory, glory as of the only begotten from the Father, full of grace and truth."

Fulfillment – Matthew 1:22-23

Now all this took place to fulfill what was spoken by the Lord through the prophet: "Behold, the virgin shall be with child and shall bear a Son, and they shall call His name 'Immanuel,' which translated means, 'God with us'" (Matt. 1:22-23).

If there were no other evidence to be found concerning the messianic nature of Isaiah 7:14, this passage from the hand of Matthew would stand alone as sufficient proof. After relating the miraculous circumstances surrounding the conception of Jesus, Matthew stated, "Now all this took place that what was spoken by the Lord through the prophet might be fulfilled . . . "

3. Preceded By a Messenger – Isaiah 40:3

A voice is calling, "Clear the way for the Lord in the wilderness; make smooth in the desert a highway for our God" (Isa. 40:3).

(I have chosen to include this prophecy even though the primary subject of it is not the Messiah; rather one who was to come before Him. As we will see, it has reference to John the Baptist, a cousin of the Lord who preceded Him both in birth and in ministry.)

Chapter 39 of the book of Isaiah ends with a prediction of the forth-coming Babylonian Captivity that was to befall the southern kingdom of Judah. Chapter 40 begins to unfold the promise of deliverance by the hand of God. There is little question that it had a contemporary application to the deliverance from Babylonian Captivity, but that deliverance serves as a type of one much greater–the deliverance from sin and death by the Savior. In both cases the coming salvation was announced by a herald. The prophecy reaches its ultimate fulfillment in the person of John the Baptist.

Let's notice comments concerning the prophecy by other writers.

From Matthew Henry's *Commentary in One Volume*:

The time to favour Zion having come, the people of God must be prepared, by repentance and faith, for the favours designed for them. We have here the voice of one crying in the wilderness, which may be applied to those prophets, with the captives, who, when they saw the day of their deliverance dawn, called earnestly upon them to prepare for it. But it must be applied to John the Baptist; for, though God was the speaker, he was the voice of one crying in the wilderness to prepare the way of the Lord, to dispose men's minds for the reception of the gospel of Christ (882-883).

From E.W. Hengstenberg's *Christology of the Old Testament*:

The deliverance from Babylon is clearly predicted, but at the same time it is employed as an image to designate a deliverance of an infinitely higher and more important character. As Isaiah scarcely ever speaks of the inferior deliverance without alluding to the higher, so is it here. It is only through the Messiah, that the prediction of the forgiveness of sins, of the restoration of the people, of the manifestation of the glory of God, will be fulfilled in its highest and most complete sense. This concurrent reference to the higher deliverance is proved, partly by the nature of prophecy itself, and partly by the most distinct passages of the New Testament. In these passages, the third verse is referring to John the Baptist. He was called to remove the obstacles which retarded the revelation of the glory of God in the Messiah; he occupied the first place among the heralds, who prepared the way of the great king (382).

Fulfillment – Matthew 3:1-3

Now in those days John the Baptist came, preaching in the wilderness of Judea, saying, "Repent, for the kingdom of heaven is at hand." For this is the one referred to by Isaiah the prophet when he said, "The voice of one crying in the wilderness, make ready the way of the Lord, make His paths straight!" (Matt. 3:1-3).

Foy E. Wallace Jr. once wrote, "The only infallible interpretation of prophecy is an inspired interpretation" (*God's Prophetic Word*, 64). The first three verses of the third chapter in Matthew's gospel leave no doubt as to the meaning of the prophecy found in Isaiah 40:3. It referred to John the Baptist.

Other passages such as Mark 1:1-6 and Luke 3:1-6 help us to identify "those days." Tiberius was the Roman emperor; Pontius Pilate was governor of Judea; Herod Antipas was the tetrarch of Galilee; his brother Philip was tetrarch of Ituraea and Trachonitis; and Lysanias was the tetrarch of Abilene. "Tetrarch" means "ruler of a fourth part of a country." Annas and Caiaphas were the high priests. Annas was the rightful high priest, but he had been removed by the procurator, Gratus, in A.D. 14. Caiaphas was his son-in-law, and had been appointed in his place.

In "those days," John came preaching in the wilderness of Judea. This was an area of land located along the western side of the Dead Sea and a small strip of land to the north of the Dead Sea. John's primary message was one of repentance, "for the kingdom of heaven" was at hand. Multitudes responded to John's call to the "baptism of repentance for the remission of sins." While his purpose was to prepare the way for the coming Messiah, his baptism was "for the remission of sins." I believe that those sincerely baptized with John's baptism had their sins forgiven in the same way a devout Jew had his sins forgiven on the Day of Atonement. Confronted by the full gospel of our Lord Jesus they would have to respond in obedience and be baptized into the death of the Lord. The twelve men that we read about in Acts 19:1-7 are an example of this.

There are certain differences between the baptism of John and the baptism in the name of Jesus that should be considered. (1) The baptism in the name of Jesus is final. It is the "one baptism" of Ephesians 4. John's baptism was temporary. (2) The baptism in the name of Jesus is "into Christ." John's baptism was preparatory. (3) The baptism in the name of Jesus is into the death of Christ. At the time of John's baptism, Jesus had not yet died. (4) One baptized with the baptism of Jesus receives the "gift of the Holy Spirit" (Acts 2:38). There was no such promise connected to John's baptism. (5) The baptism in the name of Jesus is offered to, and is necessary for, everyone. John's baptism was only to the Jews.

John's appearance and his message were in fulfillment of prophecy. John's task was to remove the obstacles, to herald the coming of the Messiah, to prepare His path. This man, the son of Zacharias and Elizabeth and the cousin of the Lord, fulfilled his mission.

4. Born at Bethlehem – Micah 5:2

But as for you, Bethlehem Ephrathah, too little to be among the clans of Judah, from you One will go forth for Me to be ruler in Israel. His goings forth are from long ago, from the days of eternity (Mic. 5:2).

It is not difficult to determine the meaning of this prophecy for we have inspired passages that tell us how the Jews understood it, and their understanding was correct. The small village of Bethlehem Ephrathah was destined to be the birthplace of the King of the Jews, the coming Messiah. That this was the view held by the Jews during the time of Jesus is clearly pointed out in Matthew 2:3-6, "And when Herod the king heard it, he was troubled, and all Jerusalem with him. And gathering together all the chief priests and scribes of the people, he began to inquire of them where the Christ was to be born. And they said to him, 'In Bethlehem of Judea, for so it has been written by the prophet, And you, Bethlehem, land of Judah, are by no means least among the leaders of Judah; for out of you shall come forth a Ruler, Who will shepherd My people Israel.'"

Of the response of the chief priests and scribes to Herod's question concerning the birthplace of the Christ, McGarvey and Pendleton wrote, "The use which the scribes made of this prophecy is very important, for it shows that the Jews originally regarded this passage of Scripture as fixing the birthplace of Messiah, and condemns as a fruit of bigotry and prejudice the modern effort of certain rabbis to explain away this natural interpretation" (*The Fourfold Gospel*, 46).

That this view was generally held by the Jewish populace and not just the chief priests and scribes can be seen in John 7:40-42, "Some of the multitude therefore, when they heard these words, were saying, This certainly is the Prophet. Others were saying, This is the Christ. Still others were saying, Surely the Christ is not going to come from Galilee, is He? Has not the Scripture said that the Christ comes from the offspring of David, and from Bethlehem, the village where David was?"

Fulfillment – Luke 2:4-7

Joseph also went up from Galilee, from the city of Nazareth, to Judea, to the city of David which is called Bethlehem, because he was of the house and family of David, in order to register along with Mary, who was engaged to him, and was with child. While they were there, the days were completed for her to give birth. And she gave birth to her firstborn son; and she wrapped Him in cloths, and laid Him in a manger, because there was no room for them in the inn (Luke 2:4-7).

Joseph and Mary, both of the lineage of David, and Mary about to be delivered of a child, made their way to Bethlehem, the city of David, to be enrolled. As I envision this scene of the humble carpenter and his pregnant wife making the arduous eighty mile journey from Nazareth to Bethlehem for enrollment in the city of their great ancestor, I am reminded of Isaiah 11:1. There we find, "Then a shoot will spring from the stem of Jesse, and a branch from his roots will bear fruit." The world did not know that the house of David, referred to as "the stem of Jesse," cut down and brought low as evidenced by the poverty and obscurity of Joseph and Mary, was about to have the Branch spring forth of it and be raised to greater heights than it had ever known during the time of David or Solomon. While in the city of David, Jesus was born. No more humble surroundings could be imagined. Our Lord was born in a stable because the enrollment had brought a large number of people to Bethlehem and there was no room for them in the inn. His first bed was a manger.

Jamieson, Fausset and Brown make an interesting statement concerning the fulfillment of this prophecy in their *Commentary on the Whole Bible*: "Mary had up to this time been living at the wrong place for the Messiah's birth. A little longer stay at Nazareth, and the prophecy would have failed. But lo! With no intention certainly on her part, much less of Caesar Augustus, to fulfill the prophecy, she is brought from Nazareth to Bethlehem, and at that nick of time her period arrives, and her Babe is born" (991).

As we examine prophecies such as this and see how they came to be fulfilled, we cannot help but marvel at the infinite wisdom and incredible power of God.

5. Called Immanuel – Isaiah 7:14

Therefore the Lord Himself will give you a sign: Behold, a virgin will be with child and bear a son, and she will call His name Immanuel (Isa. 7:14).

We have already examined one aspect of this prophecy but would like to turn our attention to another. This child, who was to be born of a virgin, would be called "Immanuel" or "God with us." Immediately our thoughts turn to yet another prophecy found in Isaiah 9:6, in which we are told that the child would be called, "Wonderful Counselor, Mighty God, Eternal Father, Prince of Peace." There is no other to whom the title "Immanuel" can be appropriately applied than Jesus.

Fulfillment – Matthew 1:22-23, John 1:14

Now all this took place to fulfill what was spoken by the Lord through the prophet: Behold, the virgin shall be with child and shall bear a Son, and they shall call His name "Immanuel," which translated means "God with us" (Matt. 1:22-23).

And the Word became flesh, and dwelt among us, and we saw His glory, glory as of the only begotten from the Father, full of grace and truth (John 1:14).

The promise of "God with us" came to pass in the city of Bethlehem so many years ago, when the Lord was born. It is a fundamental teaching of the New Testament that Jesus was both God and man. He is the only one about whom such a truth can be taught.

We are considering the Incarnation, a truly incredible idea to contemplate. God was made flesh and tabernacled among men. Jesus was deity in the flesh, visible and tangible, walking the streets of the world that He had created. When He came, men beheld His glory.

In the Old Testament, the "glory" of God abode in the Tabernacle. Exodus 40:34-35 describes that beautiful picture. With the coming of Jesus, God took up residence among men, and mankind was privileged to behold His glory. The uniqueness of the situation is indicated by "the only begotten from the Father." The Incarnation was absolutely unique; nothing like it had occurred before and nothing like it has occurred since. In 1 Timothy 3:16 Paul wrote, "By common confession, great is the mystery of godliness: He who was revealed in the flesh, was vindicated in the Spirit, seen by angels, proclaimed among the nations, believed on in the world, taken up in glory."

6. Called Lord – Psalm 110:1

The Lord says to my Lord: Sit at My right hand, until I make Your enemies a footstool for Your feet (Psa. 110:1).

The meaning of this prophetic statement is made clear by the use Jesus made of it in Matthew 22:41-46. Not only is its actual meaning shown in that passage, but the generally held view concerning it by the Jews in Jesus' time can be seen as well.

In Matthew 22:41-46 we read:

Now while the Pharisees were gathered together, Jesus asked them a question: "What do you think about the Christ, whose son is He?" They said to Him, "The son of David." He said to them, "Then how does David in the Spirit call Him, 'Lord,' saying, 'The Lord said to my Lord, sit at My right hand, until I put Your enemies beneath Your feet?' If David then calls Him, 'Lord,' how is He his son?" No one was able to answer Him a word, nor did anyone dare from that day on to ask Him another question.

Jesus Himself applied this prophecy to the Messiah. Had it been viewed as an erroneous application of this passage by Jesus, the Pharisees could have, and certainly would have, taken the opportunity to point out His error. Their silence indicates that they also viewed this prophecy as relating to the Messiah. The psalm was written by David, and neither David himself, nor any other person but the Messiah, could be its subject. What other man could King David consistently call his Lord?

An interesting statement is found in Spurgeon's *The Treasury of David*. It is a quote by Robert Abbot in *The Exaltation of the Kingdom and Priesthood of Christ*. Abbot wrote:

> Although the Jews of later times have gone about to wrest it to another meaning, yet this Psalm is so approved and undoubted a prophecy of Christ, that the Pharisees durst not deny it, when being questioned by our Savior (Matthew 22:42-43) how it should be, seeing Christ is the son of David, that David notwithstanding should call him Lord, saying, 'The Lord said unto my Lord,' they could not answer him a word, whereas the answer had been very easy and ready if they could have denied this psalm to be meant of Christ. But they knew it could not be otherwise understood, and it was commonly taken amongst them to be a prophecy of their Messiah, according to the very evidence of the text itself, which cannot be fitted to any other, but only to Christ our Savior, the Son of God (I: 191).

Fulfillment – Acts 2:34-36, Luke 2:10-11

For it was not David who ascended into heaven, but he himself says: "The Lord said to my Lord, 'Sit at My right hand, until I make Your enemies a footstool for Your feet.'" Therefore let all the house of Israel know for certain that God has made Him both Lord and Christ–this Jesus whom you crucified (Acts 2:34-36).

* Luke 2:10-11 demonstrates its fulfillment as well in the announcement of the birth of Jesus to the shepherds in the field.*

But the angel said to them, "Do not be afraid; for behold, I bring you good news of great joy which will be for all the people; for today in the city of David there has been born for you a Savior, who is Christ the Lord" (Luke 2:10-11).

Why appear to shepherds? There is significance to this. First, they were Jews, but why not appear to the scholars in Jerusalem, or the elders of the people? Why not announce the birth to the influential Jewish leaders? Interestingly, at this time shepherds were held in low esteem by the people. According to the Talmud in the treatise *"The Sanhedrin,"* shepherds were not permitted to be used in courts as witnesses. Why appear to men of such low estate?

I believe it was to demonstrate the very nature of Christianity. It is for all men, from the least to the greatest, recognizing no class distinction in terms of the love of God and the availability of salvation. It was as Mary said in the Magnificat, "He has brought down rulers from their thrones, and has exalted those who were humble" (Luke 1:52).

Some comments concerning "Lord" are appropriate. The word "Lord" (*Kurios*) as a noun, is translated in the New Testament in various ways, such as "master," "owner," even "sir." But I want to notice what W.E. Vine says of it in his *Expository Dictionary of New Testament Words*:

Christ Himself assumed the title, Matthew 7:21, 22; 9:38; 22:41-45; Mark 5:19 (cp. Psalms 66:16; the parallel passage, Luke 8:39, has 'God'); Luke 19:31; John 13:13, apparently intending it in the higher senses of its current use, and at the same time suggesting its O.T. associations.

His purpose did not become clear to the disciples until after His resurrection, and the revelation of His Deity consequent thereon. Thomas, when he realized the significance of the presence of a mortal wound in the body of a living man, immediately joined with it the absolute title of Deity, saying, "My Lord and my God," John 20:28. Thereafter, except in Acts 10:4 and Revelation 7:14, there is no record that *kurios* was ever again used by believers in addressing any save God and the Lord Jesus; cp. Acts 2:47 with 4:29-30.

How soon and how completely the lower meaning had been superceded is seen in Peter's declaration in his first sermon after the resurrection, "God hath made Him – Lord," Acts 2:36 (III: 16-17).

7. Presented With Gifts – Psalm 72:10, 12-15

Let the kings of Tarshish and of the islands bring presents; the kings of Sheba and Seba offer gifts. . . .For he will deliver the needy when he cries for help, the afflicted also, and him who has no helper. He will have compassion on the poor and needy, and the lives of the needy he will save. He will rescue their life from oppression and violence; and their blood will be precious in his sight; so may he live, and may the gold of Sheba be given to him; and let them pray for him continually; let them bless him all day long (Psa. 72:10, 12-15).

Actually, verse 10 is the specific verse that I want to notice; however, I included verses 12-15 because they amplify the Messianic nature of the prophecy.

Many believe that Psalm 72:10 had historical application to King Solomon and cite 2 Chronicles 9:1, 23-24:

Now when the queen of Sheba heard of the fame of Solomon, she came to Jerusalem to test Solomon with difficult questions. She had a very large retinue, with camels carrying spices and a large amount of gold and precious stones; and when she came to Solomon, she spoke with him about all that was on her heart. . . .And all the kings of the earth were seeking the presence of Solomon, to hear his wisdom which God had put in his heart. They brought every man his gift, articles of silver and gold, garments, weapons, spices, horses and mules, so much year by year.

I certainly would not deny historical application to Solomon, yet at the same time I realize that "the testimony of Jesus is the spirit of prophecy" (Rev. 19:10). In examining verses 12-15 of the psalm we realize that much of what is written cannot have a Solomonic application. Hengstenberg makes an interesting statement concerning this prophecy:

The non-Messianic interpreters seek to show the fulfillment from the tenth chapter of the first book of Kings, according to which the Queen of Sheba, and others also, brought costly presents to Solomon. But though we would not wish to deny that this writer, in his figurative representation, had these transactions in view, we must, never-theless, assert, that they are by no means a fulfillment of the prophetic language of the Psalm. What is said is far too great for Solomon. . . . Over all these nations this king shall reign, and they shall serve Him with the deepest humility. Every difficulty is removed by the reference to the Messiah" (*Christology of the Old Testament*, 61).

Fulfillment – Matthew 2:1-2, 11

Now after Jesus was born in Bethlehem of Judea in the days of Herod the king, magi from the east arrived in Jerusalem, saying, "Where is He who has been born King of the Jews? For we saw His star in the east and have come to worship Him." . . .After coming into the house they saw the Child with Mary His mother; and they fell to the ground and worshiped Him. Then opening their treasures, they presented to Him gifts of gold, frankincense, and myrrh (Matt. 2:1-2, 11).

The original word used for *magi* is the word from which we get "magician." While there may be a somewhat negative connotation to that word today, or at least to the idea of an illusionist, it was not so originally. These were learned men of eastern nations, principally Persia and Arabia. They were devoted to the study of astronomy, religion, and medicine. They were held in high regard and sought after as counselors.

It is apparent that, at this time, there was a prevalent expecta-tion in the east that some remarkable personage was to appear in Judea. There were Jews living in all parts of the known world and as they spread, they took their expectations of a Messiah with them. Mention of this expectation appears in different secular works of the time. Seutonius, a Roman historian, wrote, "An ancient and settled persuasion prevailed throughout the East, that the Fates had decreed someone to proceed from Judea, who should attain universal em-pire" (*Vespasian*, 4). Yet another Roman historian, Tacitus, wrote, "Many were persuaded that it was contained in the ancient books of their priests, that at that very time the East should prevail, and that some one should proceed from Judea and possess the dominion" (*Annals*, 5, 13).

Ancient astrologers often considered the appearance of a star or comet as an omen of some remarkable event. These magi were no different. It is important to note that none of the theories set forth to give a natural explanation of the appearance of this star do so. They all fall short. This was a miraculous occurrence.

From *The International Standard Bible Encyclopedia* we find that the inhabitants of Seba and Sheba were in Arabia, or the east. Gold, and particularly frankincense (the fragrant gum of a tree obtained by cutting the bark) and myrrh (also from trees and used chiefly in the embalming of the dead), were products of Arabia. So these men from Seba and Sheba came bearing gifts as prophesied in Psalm 72:10, these "magi from the east," and the prophecy was fulfilled.

8. Herod Has the Children Murdered – Jeremiah 31:15

Thus says the Lord, "A voice is heard in Ramah, lamentation and bitter weeping. Rachel is weeping for her children; she refuses to be comforted for her children, because they are no more" (Jer. 31:15).

In order to properly understand this prophecy, it is necessary to view it contextually and realize that Jeremiah speaks of the carrying away into Babylonian captivity as well as the restoration of all of God's people as one nation. Jamieson, Fausett, and Brown tell us:

Ramah – In Benjamin, east of the great northern road, two hours' journey (on foot, GL) from Jerusalem. Rachel, who all her life had pined for children (Genesis 30:1), and who died with "sorrow" in giving birth to Benjamin, and was buried at Ramah, near Bethlehem, is represented as raising her head from the tomb, and as breaking forth into "weeping" at seeing the whole land depopulated of her sons, the Ephraimites. Ramah was the place where Nebuzaradan collected all the Jews in chains, previous to their removal to Babylon (*Commentary on the Whole Bible*, 634).

This, however, is not what the prophecy ultimately referred to. Matthew 2:16-18 gives us the divine interpretation of its meaning.

Fulfillment – Matthew 2:16-18

Then when Herod saw that he had been tricked by the magi, he became very enraged, and sent and slew all the male children who were in Bethlehem and in all its vicinity, from two years old and under, according to the time which he had determined from the magi. Then what had been spoken through Jeremiah the prophet was fulfilled: "A voice was heard in Ramah, weeping and great mourning, Rachel weeping for her children; and she refused to be comforted, because they were no more" (Matt. 2:16-18).

This Herod was Herod the Great who was visited by the magi and asked, "Where is He who has been born King of the Jews? For we saw His star in the east, and have come to worship Him." His reaction to the visit of the magi and their purpose for coming is not surprising. This was a man who had already executed several of his relatives whom he viewed as possible threats to his throne. News of these events agitated Herod, as yet another possible usurper to his position was born. He knew of the expectation of the Messiah and he knew that the Jews expected a temporal king, so he gathered together the chief priests and the scribes to inquire where they looked for the Christ to be born. The answer was Bethlehem of Judea.

The next step Herod took to eliminate the possible threat was to summon the magi to him privately and to seek to learn the time of the appearance of the star. This he did to ascertain the age of the child. Having done so, he sent the magi to Bethlehem to look for the baby, telling them that after they found Him, they were to return to Herod and give him word of the child's whereabouts that he might worship Him as well. When Herod saw that the magi did not return as he had expected, he was very angry. He issued orders that all the male children, two years old and under, in Bethlehem and the regions surrounding it, were to be executed. He did this to be certain that he had killed the right child. As is so often the case in Scripture, evil men, totally unbeknownst to themselves, behave in such a way as to bring about the fulfillment of prophecy. Such was the case with Herod the Great's intention to kill Jesus.

While experience should teach me not to be, I must admit to being surprised each time I find one who claims to be a believer in the Word of God, deny a clear statement of scripture. Such was the case as I researched this prophecy. While Matthew plainly says the killing of the children by order of Herod fulfilled the prophecy of Jeremiah 31:15, William Barclay saw fit to disagree. Barclay wrote, "The verse in Jeremiah has no connection with Herod's slaughter of the children. . . . Matthew is doing what he so often did. In his eagerness he is finding a prophecy where no prophecy is" (*The Gospel of Matthew*, I: 38). To do such, an individual must either deny the divine, plenary inspiration of Scripture, or believe that God made a mistake. Neither choice is acceptable or logical.

9. Called Out of Egypt – Hosea 11:1

When Israel was a youth I loved him, and out of Egypt I called My son (Hos. 11:1).

In Exodus 4:22 we find the children of Israel collectively referred to in the following fashion: "Israel is My son." God greatly loved His "son" and looked down upon the Israelites with compassion because of the cruel Egyptian bondage under which they were living. He sent relief, using Moses as their leader, to deliver His son, Israel, from Egypt. From an historical standpoint, it can be said that the statement of Hosea 11:1 looked back to that time. However, the statement also looked to a time some 750 years later when the unique Son of God, our Lord Jesus, would be leaving Egypt to go to Israel. It looked forward to a time when another wicked king, Herod the Great instead of Pharaoh, would be seeking to destroy His Son.

Fulfillment – Matthew 2:13-15

Now when they had gone, behold, an angel of the Lord appeared to Joseph in a dream and said, "Get up! Take the Child and His mother and flee to Egypt, and remain there until I tell you; for Herod is going to search for the Child to destroy Him." So Joseph got up and took the Child and His mother while it was still night, and left for Egypt. He remained there until the death of Herod. This was to fulfill what had been spoken by the Lord through the prophet: "Out of Egypt I called My Son" (Matt. 2:13-15).

Why Egypt? (1) Obviously it was in fulfillment of prophecy; (2) Egypt was only about 60 miles southwest of Bethlehem, and there was certainly a precedent for troubled Jews going to Egypt; (3) Herod's jurisdiction ended at the River of Egypt, so Joseph and his family would be safe there. But the prophecy is much deeper than it might appear on its surface.

In Genesis 12:14-20, Abraham went down into Egypt because of a famine in Canaan. In Moses' description of these events, he used wording that echoed the events of the Exodus. Abraham goes down into Egypt and is well received. When Pharaoh takes Sarai for his wife, God "plagues" Pharaoh and Egypt for her sake. Circumstances change for Pharaoh and he is driven from the country. However, he departs with many goods.

During the life of Jacob, Israel migrates to Egypt where they are happily received, because of the work of Joseph. But, a new Pharaoh rises up who does not know Joseph and Israel's circumstances change. Israel becomes slaves in Egypt. Because of how Israel is treated, God calls up "his son" from Egyptian bondage. Plagues are sent upon Egypt for Israel's sake and, after the tenth plague, Egypt drives Israel out of the land of Egypt (Exod. 12:29-35). But, like Abraham before them, Israel spoiled the Egyptians as they departed Egypt (Exod. 12:35-36). Just as Abraham went down into Egypt and came up out of Egypt, so did Israel.

Both of these events prefigure what happened to God's Son. Because of Herod's massacre of the infants, Joseph was instructed by God to take his son and flee into Egypt. After Herod the Great's death, Joseph, Mary, and Jesus came out of Egypt. The God, who controlled the events of Abraham and Israel, used those events to foreshadow what He would cause to occur in the birth of His Son. God's hand was in human history on all three occasions to foretell, first the circumstance of Israel's sojourn in Egypt, and then of the sojourn of the Son of God in Egypt.

Chapter Three

Prophecies Concerning His Lineage

We now turn our attention to prophecies pertaining to the lineage of the Messiah. They play an extremely important role as the picture of the Promised One unfolds in the pages of the Old Testament, becoming continuously clearer and more specific. To the Jews, these prophecies concerning the Messiah's lineage were vital. Of the word "lineage" itself, the *International Bible Encyclopedia* states, "A word pregnant in meaning among the Jews, who kept all family records with religious care, as may be seen from the long genealogical records found everywhere in the Old Testament" (III: 1894).

These prophecies served to prove that Jesus was the Messiah for whom the Jews had waited. He was the Son of David. He was of the line of Abraham. The prophecies, and their fulfillment, "become proofs of the Messiahship of Jesus. Prophecy fixed one condition. The Messiah would belong to the royal house of David. Now observe that during Christ's life this was never once disputed. The Sanhedrin kept the public archives; and though Herod the Great sought out and burnt all the family registers he could, the enemies of Christ never attempted to disprove He claims to belong to the royal race . . . .Ulla, a rabbi of the third century, says, 'Jesus was treated in an exceptional way, because he was of the royal race'" (*The Pulpit Commentary*, XV: 25).

We, many centuries later, can examine these prophecies, trace the lineage of the Promised One, and take great comfort as we see them fulfilled in our Lord and Savior.

1. Son of God – Psalm 2:7

I will surely tell of the decree of the Lord: He said to Me, "You are My Son, today I have begotten You" (Psa. 2:7).

The entire second Psalm is Messianic. Couched in the phrases and war-like images of David's reign, it prophesied of the kingdom of Jesus. Many times the New Testament writers refer to this psalm, and specifically verse 7, applying it to our Lord. Instances of such usage are found in Acts 13:33 as Paul taught in the synagogue in Antioch of Pisidia, as well as in Hebrews 1:5.

That this psalm, and particularly verse 7, was viewed by the Jews of Jesus' time as Messianic cannot be disputed. Hengestenberg, in *Christology of the Old Testament*, says of it:

> It is an undoubted fact, and unanimously admitted even by the recent opposers of its reference to Him, that the Psalm was universally regarded by the ancient Jews as foretelling the Messiah. The high priest asked Jesus, whether He were the Christ, the Son of God: thus borrowing from it two appellations of the expected Redeemer; and also Nathanael said to Christ with reference to this Psalm, "Thou art the Son of God: thou art the King of Israel." In the older Jewish writings also there is a variety of passages in which the Messianic interpretation is given to this psalm. Even Kimchi and Jarchi confess, that it was the prevailing one among their forefathers; and the latter very honestly gives his reason for departing from it, when he says he preferred to explain it of David for the refutation of the heretics, that is, in order to destroy the force of the argument drawn from it by the Christians (43-44).

So the promised King would be the Son of God—of the same nature as His Father and Heir of all things.

Fulfillment – Matthew 3:16-17

After being baptized, Jesus came up immediately from the water; and behold, the heavens were opened, and he saw the Spirit of God descending as a dove and lighting on Him, and behold, a voice out of the heavens said, "This is My beloved Son, in whom I am well-pleased" (Matt. 3:16-17).

This is a title that God the Father applies to Jesus, a title that He had indicated would be His in Psalm 2:7. It signifies the shared nature, the dignity and the love of the Father and the Son. Truly to none other was the title, "My beloved Son," applied. Perhaps there is also reference here to the unique circumstances of our Lord's birth. He was "of the seed of woman," yes, but not of man. He was, as none other, the Son of God.

Later Jesus would refer to Himself as the Son of God, and the religious leaders of the time understood what Jesus was actually saying. Consider John 5:17-25:

> But He answered them, "My Father is working until now, and I Myself am working." For this reason therefore the Jews were seeking all the more to kill Him, because He not only was breaking the Sabbath, but also was calling God His own Father, making Himself equal with God. Therefore Jesus answered and was saying to them, "Truly, truly, I say to you, the Son can do nothing of Himself, unless it is something He sees the Father doing; for whatever the Father does, these things the Son also does in like manner. For the Father loves the Son, and shows Him all things that He Himself is doing; and the Father will show Him greater works than these, that you will marvel. For just as the Father raises the dead and gives them life, even so the Son also gives life to whom He wishes. For not even the Father judges anyone, but He has given all judgment to the Son, so that all will honor the Son even as they honor the Father. He who does not honor the Son does not honor the Father who sent Him. Truly, truly, I say to you, he who hears My word, and believes Him who sent Me, has eternal life, and does not come into judgment, but has passed out of death into life. Truly, truly, I say to you, an hour is coming and now is, when the dead will hear the voice of the Son of God, and those who hear will live."

In John 10:30 Jesus said, "I and the Father are one." By referring to Himself as the Son of God and by saying that He and His Father were one, Jesus was saying that they possessed the divine nature equally. There are those today who say that Jesus never claimed to be God – but the leaders of the Jews of that time knew exactly what Jesus was saying. They thought they had what they needed to put

Him to death–blasphemy–because the Lord's statement was in fact an assertion of divinity.

2. Seed of Abraham – Genesis 12:2-3, 22:17-18

And I will make you a great nation, and I will bless you, and make your name great; and so you shall be a blessing; and I will bless those who bless you, and the one who curses you I will curse. And in you all the families of the earth will be blessed (Gen. 12:2-3).

Indeed I will greatly bless you, and I will greatly multiply your seed as the stars of the heavens and as the sand which is on the seashore; and your seed shall possess the gate of their enemies. In your seed all the nations of the earth shall be blessed, because you have obeyed My voice (Gen. 22:17-18).

The initial call and promise to Abraham are recorded in Genesis 12. Several years later, after Abraham had demonstrated his faithfulness to God through obedience to His commands, God renewed the promise. In verse 17 of Genesis 22, the word "seed" is used to refer to Abraham's posterity, the whole nation of Israel. However, in verse 18 it is greatly limited. In verse 18 it refers to one specific descendant of Abraham, Jesus the Christ.

Notice what Matthew Henry wrote concerning the phrase "in your seed" of verse 18 in his *Commentary in One Volume*. He wrote, "In thy seed, one particular person that shall descend from thee (for he speaks not of many, but of one, as the apostle observes, Galatians 3:16), shall all the nations of the earth be blessed."

Thus it was determined by God that the Messiah was to be a descendant of Abraham. While the Promised One would be Jewish, the blessings made possible through Him would not be limited to the Jewish race, but would be open to all people.

Fulfillment – Matthew 1:1 and Galatians 3:16

The record of the genealogy of Jesus the Messiah, the son of David, the son of Abraham (Matt. 1:1).

Now the promises were spoken to Abraham and to his seed. He does not say, "And to seeds," as referring to many, but rather to one, "And to your seed," that is, Christ (Gal. 3:16).

I referred to Matthew 1:1 simply to demonstrate that Jesus was of the seed of Abraham. Galatians 3:16 addresses the promise made to Abraham directly and acts as a divine interpretation concerning the meaning of the word "seed" in Genesis 22:18. There is no question that it referred to Jesus and finds its fulfillment in Him.

Of Galatians 3:1, James Macknight wrote in his *Apostolic Epistles*:

He proceeds in this passage to consider the promise made to Abraham's seed, that in it likewise all nations of the earth should be blessed. And from the words of the promise, which are not "and in thy seeds," but "and in thy seed," he argues that the seed in which the nations of the earth should be blessed, is not Abraham's seed in general, but one of his seeds, in particular, namely Christ; who by dying for all nations, hath delivered them from the curse of the law, that the blessing of justification by faith might come on believers of all nations through Christ, as was promised to Abraham (292).

3. Son of Isaac – Genesis 21:12
But God said to Abraham, "Do not be distressed because of the lad and your maid; whatever Sarah tells you, listen to her, for through Isaac your descendants shall be named" (Gen. 21:12).

Very little needs to be said of this prophecy except to notice how it fits into the development of God's plans. We have already noticed that the Messiah was to be a descendant of Abraham. Abraham was the father of two sons, Ishmael by Hagar and Isaac by Sarah. With this prophecy, one half of the lineage of Abraham is eliminated.

Fulfillment – Matthew 1:1-2
The record of the genealogy of Jesus the Messiah, the son of David, the son of Abraham: Abraham was the father of Isaac; Isaac the father of Jacob, and Jacob the father of Judah and his brothers (Matt. 1:1-2).

A valid question to consider is "Why study the genealogies?" We see its validity when we consider the amount of space devoted to them in Matthew and Luke. The answer is readily apparent. In the infancy of the church the genealogies played a role of great importance. We get an idea of their significance from an exchange that we find in Matthew 22:41-42. It says, "Now while the Pharisees were gathered together, Jesus asked them a question: 'What do you think about the Christ, whose son is He?' They said to Him, 'The son of David.'"

The Jews of the first century knew that the Messiah was to be of the lineage of David. They were well versed in such passages as 2 Samuel 7:12-16, Psalm 89:3-4 and Psalm 132:11. The genealogies trace Jesus back to David and solidly connect Him with the Messianic prophecies.

Isn't it interesting that Matthew begins his account of Jesus by establishing this fact? Surely that demonstrates the importance of Jesus' ancestry, especially in a gospel that was evidently written to the Jewish mind. Luke includes his genealogical record of Jesus immediately following our Lord's baptism and just prior to the beginning of His public ministry. The fact that Luke's gospel was written to be read primarily by Gentiles, and includes the genealogy, demonstrates that it was of universal interest and importance. Today we have the benefit of centuries past, and recognize the ancestry of Jesus as proven. The first century Christians did not have this advantage and needed to be properly prepared to teach the Messiahship of Jesus in light of Old Testament prophecy.

Matthew's genealogy is the shorter of the two. It goes from Abraham forward forty-two generations, ending with "Joseph the husband of Mary, by whom was born Jesus, who is called the Messiah." It is divided into three groups of fourteen each, the first being from Abraham to David, the second from David to the Babylonian Captivity, and the third being from the Captivity to Jesus.

What Matthew was doing needs to be considered. Not only was he demonstrating the connection of Jesus to David, he was also supplying an abbreviated history lesson. He traces the origin of the house of David from Abraham to David. He shows its rise to power and its decay from David to the Captivity, and he shows how it rose again as promised from the Captivity to Jesus. There is a definite historical movement to Matthew's genealogy that demonstrates a twofold purpose. Matthew was connecting the ancestry of Jesus to David, and he was tracing the rise, fall, and rise again of the house of David.

4. Son of Jacob – Genesis 28:13-14 and Numbers 24:17

And behold, the Lord stood above it and said, "I am the Lord, the God of your father Abraham and the God of Isaac; the land on which you lie, I will give it to you and to your descendants. Your descendants will also be like the dust of the earth, and you will spread out to the west and to the east and to the north and to the south; and in you and in your descendants shall all the families of the earth be blessed" (Gen. 28:13-14).

I see him, but not now; I behold him, but not near; a star shall come forth from Jacob, a scepter shall rise from Israel, and shall crush through the forehead of Moab, and tear down all the sons of Sheth (Num. 24:17).

Isaac had fathered twin sons, with Rebekah. They were Jacob and Esau. With the prophecy of Genesis 28:13-14, one half of the lineage of Isaac was eliminated as far as the Messiah was concerned. Of the statement made to Jacob in verses thirteen and fourteen of Genesis 28, Matthew Henry writes in his *Commentary in One Volume*:

The former promises made to his father were repeated and ratified to him. In general, God intimated to him that he would be the same to him that he had been to Abraham and Isaac. The land of Canaan is settled upon him. It is promised him that his posterity would multiply exceedingly as the dust of the earth. It is added that the Messiah should come forth of his loins, in whom all the families of the earth should be blessed (48).

It is a generally held view that the "star" from Jacob mentioned in Numbers 24:17 speaks of David secondarily, and the Messiah primarily, and that it indicates that the ruler would be the "son of Jacob." While not espousing this view himself, Hengstenberg aptly describes it in *Christology of the Old Testament:*

By this Ruler, the Jews from the earliest times have understood the Messiah, either exclusively, or else principally, with a second reference to David. It is evident how widely this interpretation prevailed among the Jews, from the circumstance that the famous pseudo-Messiah, who appeared in the time of Adrian, borrowed from it the surname Bar-Chochab, Son of the Star. . . .Either its exclusive relation to the Messiah was maintained, or it was allowed to refer indeed, in the first instance, to David; but then both himself and his temporal victories were regarded as typical of Christ, and His spiritual triumphs, which (according to this exposition) the prophet had especially in view (34).

Fulfillment – Luke 3:34

The son of Jacob, the son of Isaac, the son of Abraham, the son of Terah, the son of Nahor (Luke 3:34).

Luke's genealogy is different from Matthew's. Instead of running forward from Abraham forty-two generations, it runs backward from Jesus to Adam, seventy-six generations. From Abraham to David the two genealogies are the same, but from David to Joseph they are different except for two names, Zerubbabel, and his father, Shealtiel. The major difficulty is that these two different genealogies are both presented as the line of Joseph. How do we explain it?

There are several explanations that have been offered. One is that one genealogy is giving the natural line of descent and the other the legal line of descent. It has been suggested (and this was the ancient explanation of most of the church Fathers) that Joseph was the legal son and heir of Heli, but the real son of Jacob. What seems most plausible to me is that Joseph was the son-in-law of Heli, and that Luke is actually tracing the line of Mary. This certainly would fit the character of Luke's gospel, for Luke gives more attention to the experiences of Mary than do the other gospel writers.

5. Tribe of Judah – Genesis 49:10

The scepter shall not depart from Judah, nor the ruler's staff from be- tween his feet, until Shiloh comes, and to him shall be the obedience of the peoples (Gen. 49:10).

Jacob fathered twelve sons. With the prophecy of Genesis 49:10, 11/12ths of the lineage of Jacob was eliminated from being the line through which the Messiah would come.

In order to view this in the Messianic sense, it is necessary to determine the meaning of "Shiloh" as it is used in the passage. Generally speaking, its meaning is rest – condition of peace. However, according to the wider meaning applied by the Hebrews to words signifying rest and peace, it can also include the notion of the one who brings such. In this case, a definition for the word to which no valid objection can be raised is "peacemaker." Accordingly, the older Jewish writings, including the Talmud, view the Messiah as the subject of this prophecy.

In the book, *From Creation to The Day of Eternity*, Homer Hailey wrote:

> In the promise to Judah quoted above (verse 10) Jacob prophesied that the power of kingship should not depart from Judah's lineage "until Shiloh come." This phrase is admittedly difficult, but the general meaning of "Shiloh" is "rest, condition of peace." Therefore, until there should come one whose dominion should be one of peace, the rulership would not depart from the tribe of Judah. In a personal sense it refers to the Messiah, the Prince of Peace, who would come to establish a kingdom of peace. Hence, the promise to Judah was that from his seed should come that Prince of Peace who would be the great ruler of God's kingdom. In later years Judah became the leading and ruling tribe of the nation, and through him came David, Solomon, and finally Jesus of the family of David (34-35).

Another interesting aspect of this prophecy concerns the word "scepter" and the time of its removal. The word translated "scepter" in Genesis 49:10 means "tribal staff." It denoted tribal identity. Involved in tribal identity was judicial power. This did not depart from Judah even during the time of the Babylonian Captivity (Consider Ezra 1:5, 8). When the scepter would depart from Judah, so would their judicial power.

In the book, *Jesus Before the Sanhedrin*, Magath writes, "The legal power of the Sanhedrin is restricted twenty-three years before the trial of Christ." That restriction was the loss of the legal right to pass the death sentence. It brings to mind the exchange between Pilate and the Jews recorded in John 18:29-31:

Therefore Pilate went out to them, and said, "What accusation do you bring against this Man?" They answered and said to him, "If this Man were not an evildoer, we would not have delivered Him to you." So Pilate said to them, "Take Him yourselves, and judge Him according to your law." The Jews said to him, "We are not permitted to put anyone to death."

If it had been lawful for the Jews to put a man to death at that time, Jesus would have died by stoning, not by crucifixion as prophesied.

How did the Jews of Jesus' time view the removal of their right to pronounce the death sentence? Again from the book, *Jesus Before the Sanhedrin*, we find Rabbi Rachmon saying, "When the members of the Sanhedrin found themselves deprived of their right over life and death, a general consternation took possession of them; they covered their heads with ashes, and their bodies with sackcloth, exclaiming: 'Woe unto us, for the scepter had departed from Judah, and the Messiah has not come!'"

Marvel at the workings of God. A little less than forty years after the death of Jesus, Jerusalem and the temple were destroyed, thereby eliminating the possibility of the prophesies concerning the death of our Lord being fulfilled. If He had come twenty-four years earlier, His death would have been by stoning for the scepter had not yet departed from Judah, thus removing the possibility of the prophesies concerning the manner of His death being fulfilled. But Jesus came within the necessary period of time, a period of sixty to sixty-five years.

Fulfillment – Matthew 1:2 and Hebrews 7:14

Abraham was the father of Isaac, Isaac the father of Jacob, and Jacob the father of Judah and his brothers (Matt. 1:2).

For it is evident that our Lord was descended from Judah, a tribe with reference to which Moses spoke nothing concerning priests (Heb. 7:14).

In order for Jesus to be our High Priest, there had to be a change of the priesthood. Jesus is a priest forever after the order of Melchizedek.

This also required a change of the law. Why? Because Jesus was of the tribe of Judah, a descendant of Judah, and Moses had been completely silent about men from the tribe of Judah being priests. Hence this shows us that Jesus was not only of the tribe of Judah, but that the silence of the Scriptures is prohibitive. Since Moses spoke *nothing* concerning men of the tribe of Judah being priests under the Levitical system, it meant that they were prohibited. The silence of the Scriptures still serves to authorize nothing.

6. Line of Jesse – Isaiah 11:1; Isaiah 11:10

Then a shoot will spring from the stem of Jesse, and a branch from his roots will bear fruit (Isa. 11:1).

Then in that day the nations will resort to the root of Jesse, who will stand as a signal for the peoples; and His resting place will be glorious (Isa. 11:10).

Contextually, this prophecy provides an interesting contrast. Isaiah had just foretold of the humbling of the mighty Assyrians. From their exalted state they would be brought low. The line of Jesse, which was brought low and humbled, would be exalted. This exaltation is realized in the Messiah.

The "stem of Jesse" can also be rendered "the stump of Jesse." It signifies "a trunk which had been cut down to its roots." Jesse was the father of David. An interesting question is why the Messiah here is represented as the sprout of Jesse and not of David? Hengstenberg provides the answer in *Christology of the Old Testament* when he writes, "The Prophet hereby wished to indicate that the family of David would then have so much declined, that it would be more appropriately designated after its humbler, than its royal ancestor" (187).

In his *Commentary in One Volume*, Matthew Henry says of Isaiah 11:1, "He is said to come out of Jesse rather than David, because Jesse lived and died in meanness and obscurity; his family was of small account (1 Samuel 18:18). He comes forth out of the stem, or stump, of Jesse. The house of David was reduced and brought very low at the time of Christ's birth, witness the obscurity and poverty of Joseph and Mary" (845).

Fulfillment – Matthew 1:6

Jesse was the father of David the king. David was the father of Solomon by Bathsheba who had been the wife of Uriah (Matt. 1:6).

There is little else that needs to be said as we continue to trace the line of David.

7. Son of David – 2 Samuel 7:12-16

When your days are complete and you lie down with our fathers, I will raise up your descendant after you, who will come forth from you, and I will establish his kingdom. He shall build a house for My name, and I will establish the throne of his kingdom forever. I will be a father to him and he will be a son to Me; when he commits iniquity, I will correct him with the rod of men and the strokes of the sons of men, but My lovingkindness shall not depart from him, as I took it away from Saul, whom I removed from before you. Your house and your kingdom shall endure before Me forever; your throne shall be established forever (2 Sam. 7:12-16).

Most immediately this statement applied to David's son, Solomon, and his building of the temple. But its ultimate meaning is found in Christ. In *From Creation to the Day of Eternity*, Homer Hailey wrote, "The promise of the Lord which was made first in the presence of Eve and later renewed to Abraham, Isaac, Jacob, and Judah, is growing. Abraham's seed is to be of the house of David: the kingdom of this seed of Abraham and David is to be established and He is to rule upon the throne of that kingdom forever" (36-37).

We see this promise to David repeated in other Psalms as well. For instance, Psalm 89:3-4 states, "I have made a covenant with My chosen; I have sworn to David My servant, I will establish your seed forever and build up your throne to all generations." Psalm 132:10-11 also addresses this promise: "For the sake of David Your servant, do not turn away the face of Your anointed. The Lord has sworn to David a truth from which He will not turn back; of the fruit of your body I will set upon your throne."

These prophesies were widely recognized as being Messianic.

Time and again in the Talmud the Messiah is referred to as the "Son of David."

Fulfillment – Acts 13:22-23

After He had removed him, He raised up David to be their king, concerning whom He also testified and said, "I have found David the son of Jesse, a man after My heart, who will do all My will." From the descendants of this man, according to promise, God has brought to Israel a Savior, Jesus (Acts. 13:22-23).

There are so many New Testament passages that demonstrate the fulfillment of the prophesies that the Messiah would be the Son of David–of the line of David. We could notice once again the genealogies in Matthew 1 and Luke 3, or the statement made to Mary by Gabriel in Luke 1:30-33:

Do not be afraid, Mary; for you have found favor with God. And behold, you will conceive in your womb and bear a son, and you shall name Him Jesus. He will be great, and will be called the Son of the Most High; and the Lord God will give Him the throne of His father David; and He will reign over the house of Jacob forever, and His kingdom will have no end.

We could notice the statements of Peter in Acts 2:25-33, or the statement found in Hebrews 1:5, "For to which of the angels did He ever say, 'You are My Son, today I have begotten You'? And again, 'I will be a Father to Him and He shall be a Son to Me'?" On and on we could go looking at proof that Jesus was the Son of David, but the point is clear and marvelous to contemplate. Jesus fulfilled each requirement for the lineage of the Messiah that God through the prophets had set forth.

Chapter Four

Prophecies Concerning His Ministry

The pages of the Old Testament are filled with numerous prophetic utterances concerning the work and type of ministry in which the Anointed One, the Christ, would engage. In rather remarkable detail, the spiritual nature of His work is presented, which makes the view generally held by the Jews of Jesus' time somewhat difficult to understand. The New Testament indicates that the Jews were looking for an earthly, physical king who would establish an earthly, physical kingdom. They looked for one who would forcibly throw off the shackles of the Roman oppressors and free the Jewish nation. The prophecies that we will examine in this chapter will show that no such physical king was promised, and that the work of the One Who was to come was to be primarily spiritual, not physical.

1. Prophet – Deuteronomy 18:18

I will raise up a prophet from among their countrymen like you, and I will put My words in his mouth, and he shall speak to them all that I command him (Deut. 18:18).

There are some who contend that this is a prophecy concerning an order of true prophets commissioned by the Lord to instruct His people. However, the vast majority of Bible commentators view this passage as referring primarily to the Messiah. Jamieson, Fausett and Brown tell us in their *Commentary on the Whole Bible*:

The prophet here promised was preeminently the Messiah, for He alone was "like unto Moses" in His mediatorial character; in the peculiar excellence of His ministry; in the number, variety, and magnitude of His miracles; in His close and familiar communion with God; and in His being the author of a new dispensation of religion (155).

It is not difficult to determine the generally held view of this prophecy by the Jews of Jesus' time. Many references are made to it in the New Testament. For instance, in John 6:14, after more than 5,000 had been fed with five barley loaves and two small fishes (5,000 being the number of men only), we find this statement, "Therefore when the people saw the sign which He had performed, they said, 'This is truly the Prophet who is to come into the world.'" In John 7:40 we find, "Some of the people therefore, when they heard these words, were saying, 'This certainly is the Prophet.'" It is entirely possible that the passage from Deuteronomy 18:18 is what Philip had in mind when he told Nathanael in John 1:45, "Philip found Nathanael and said to him, We have found Him of whom Moses in the Law and also the Prophets wrote – Jesus of Nazareth, the son of Joseph."

Without question the Messianic interpretation was the prevailing one among the Jews.

Fulfillment – Acts 3:22; 7:37

Moses said, "The Lord God will raise up for you a Prophet like me from your brethren; to Him you shall give heed to everything He says to you" (Acts. 3:22).

This is the Moses who said to the sons of Israel, "God will raise up for you a prophet like me from your brethren" (Acts 7:37).

Once again, the only truly infallible interpreter of prophecy is the Word of God. It is not necessary for us to wonder what Deuteronomy 18:18 referred to because Peter quoted it in his discourse in Solomon's porch located in the temple and applied it to Jesus. Likewise Stephen, before the Jewish Sanhedrin, applied it to Jesus as well in his discourse that so aroused the people that they stoned him to death. He who was to come would be a Prophet "like unto Moses," and Jesus was that Prophet.

2. Priest – Psalm 110:4

The Lord has sworn and will not change His mind, you are a priest forever according to the order of Melchizedek (Psa. 110:4).

The subject of Psalm 110 is the Priest/King who was to come. David was a king, but in no wise was he a priest of the Most High God. As the psalm indicates, this One who was to come would be a King, and at the same time a Priest. His priesthood would not be of the Aaronic or Levitical priesthood, but would be "after the order of Melchizedek." To understand the Messianic significance of this prophecy, it is necessary for us to understand something of the peculiar priesthood of Melchizedek.

We read of Melchizedek in Genesis 14:18-20. After Abram had rescued Lot we find, "And Melchizedek king of Salem brought out bread and wine; now he was a priest of God Most High. He blessed him and said, 'Blessed be Abram of God Most High, possessor of heaven and earth; and blessed be God Most High, Who has delivered your enemies into your hand.' He gave him a tenth of all."

Of Melchizedek's priesthood and the Messianic nature of Psalm 110:4, C.H. Spurgeon writes in *The Treasury of David*:

The order of Melchizedek's priesthood was the most ancient and primitive, the most free from ritual and ceremony, the most natural and simple, and at the same time the most honorable. That ancient patriarch was the father of his people, and at the same time ruled and taught them; he swayed both the scepter and the censer, reigned in righteousness, and offered sacrifice before the Lord. There has never arisen another like to him since his days. . . .Melchizedek's office was exceptional; none preceded or succeeded him; he comes upon the page of history mysteriously: no pedigree is given, no date of birth, or mention of death: he blesses Abraham, receives tithes and vanishes from the scene. . . .He is seen but once, and that once suffices. Aaron and his seed came and went; because it had no finality in it, and could never make the comers thereunto perfect (V: 188).

Melchizedek served as the type of Priest/King who was to come, and that Priest/King was Jesus.

Fulfillment – Hebrews 5:5-6; 7:1-3

So also Christ did not glorify Himself so as to become a high priest, but He who said to Him, "You are my son, today I have begotten you"; just as He says also in another passage, "You are a priest forever according to the order of Melchizedek" (Heb. 5:5-6).

For this Melchizedek, king of Salem, priest of the Most High God, who met Abraham as he was returning from the slaughter of the kings and blessed him, to whom also Abraham apportioned a tenth part of all the spoils, was first of all, by the translation of his name, king of righteousness, and then also king of Salem, which is king of peace. Without father, without mother, without genealogy, having neither beginning of days nor end of life, but made like the Son of God, he remains a priest perpetually (Heb. 7:1-3).

As we examine the prophecies and the peculiar priesthood of Jesus, there can truly be no question that Psalm 110 found its fulfillment in Jesus, the Son of God. Jesus stands as the anti-type of Melchizedek, and Spurgeon states the truth concerning this in *The Treasury of David*:

Our Lord Jesus, like Melchizedek, stands forth before us as a priest of divine ordaining; not made a priest by fleshly birth, as the sons of Aaron; he mentions neither father, mother, nor descent, as his right to the sacred office; he stands upon his personal merits, by himself alone; as no man came before him in his work, so none can follow after; his order begins and ends in his own person, and in himself it is eternal. . . . The Priest-King has been here and left his blessing upon the believing seed, and now he sits in glory in his complete character, atoning for us by the merit of his blood, and exercising all power on our behalf (V: 188).

Just as no man could take the honor of being the Jewish high priest without being properly called, so too Jesus took not the glory and honor of this position upon Himself. He was bestowed this honor and position by God the Father.

It is important to understand the significance of verse 6. One of the great mysteries of prophecy had been the apparent contradictions in some of the Messianic references. We know that some of the prophecies, such as Isaiah 9:6-7 called Him "Wonderful Counselor, Mighty God, Eternal Father, Prince of Peace," and also stated that there would be "no end to the increase of His government or of peace, on the throne of David and over His kingdom." Yet other prophecies, such as Isaiah 53:3, referred to Him as "a man of sorrows and acquainted with grief; and like one from whom men hide their face He was despised, and we did not esteem Him." Jewish scholars of the time had great difficulty reconciling these apparent contradictions and some taught that they referred to two different people – a glorious king and a suffering high priest.

The Hebrew writer explains the apparent contradiction. In chapter 1:5 he had used Psalm 110:1-2 to establish the universal kingship of Christ. In verse 4 he uses it to proclaim the universal high priesthood of Jesus, showing Him not to be of Aaron's line but a High Priest of universal dominion "after the order of Melchizedek." So we can see how the suffering High Priest and the kingly Messiah could be one and the same person.

3. King – Zechariah 6:13; 9:9

Yes, it is He who will build the temple of the Lord, and He who will bear the honor and sit and rule on His throne. Thus, He will be a priest on His throne and the counsel of peace will be between the two offices (Zech. 6:13).

Rejoice greatly, O daughter of Zion! Shout in triumph, O daughter of Jerusalem! Behold, your king is coming to you; He is just and endowed with salvation, humble, and mounted on a donkey, even on a colt, the foal of a donkey (Zech. 9:9).

These wonderful prophecies tell us so much about the Promised One. Not only do they assert His kingship but they also tell us of the nature of that kingship when compared to that of earthly kings. They truly indicate that His kingship would be unique.

In *A Commentary on the Minor Prophets*, Homer Hailey tells us:

This can look only to the Messiah's coming; there is no individual whom the higher critics have been able even plausibly to substitute. "He is just" describes not only His personal character but also the character of His rule. He would be "one that ruleth righteously, that ruleth in the fear of God" (2 Samuel 23:31). He would come bringing the full and complete salvation which Jehovah had promised so profusely, through Isaiah. The King is further described as lowly, whose lowliness is emphasized by His entering the city riding on an unbroken colt of an ass. This does not indicate the peaceful nature of His reign, but the lowliness of it in opposition to the pride and pomp of worldly kings. Since the days of Solomon, royal persons had ridden upon horses; but the character of the Messiah's kingship would be completely different. This difference in character would be demonstrated by His humble entrance upon His rule (370-371).

In the most complete and highest sense, Jesus was the promised King Who would sit upon the throne of David.

I included Zechariah 6:13 because it addresses not only the kingship of the Messiah, but also the fact that He would be a priest. This is uniquely true of Jesus. As a priest "after the order of Melchizedek," the functions of both priest and king are combined as He rules from His throne. There is none other about whom such statements could be made.

Fulfillment – Matthew 21:5; John 18:37

Say to the daughter of Zion, Behold your King is coming to you, gentle, and mounted on a donkey, even on a colt, the foal of a beast of burden (Matt. 21:5).

Therefore Pilate said to Him, "So you are a king?" Jesus answered, "You say correctly that I am a king. For this I have been born and for this I have come into the world, to testify to the truth. Everyone who is of the truth hears my voice" (John 18:37).

As we consider Matthew 21:5, the context indicates that it was now the daylight hours of Sunday. Having left Bethany, Jesus began to make His way to Jerusalem. He approached Bethphage, "the house of figs," which was a small suburb on the eastern side of the Mount of Olives, very close to Bethany. To this village, or perhaps to another very nearby, Jesus dispatched two of His disciples. We do not know which two they were.

Their instructions were clear. Jesus told them that, when they got to the village, they would find an ass and a colt (Matthew is the only one who mentions the ass) tied. They were to untie the animals and bring them to Him, and if anyone should ask what they were doing (the owner, who Luke specifically said did ask), they were to say, "The Lord has need of them." This was in fulfillment of Zechariah 9:9 and was indicative of the Lord's great humility.

This colt was to be one upon whom "no man ever yet sat." I believe that there is significance to that. The fact that it had not yet been used by man fitted it for such a sacred purpose. Consider Numbers 19:2, "This is the statute of the law which the Lord has commanded, saying, 'Speak to the sons of Israel that they bring you an unblemished red heifer in which is no defect and on which a yoke has never been placed.'" This certainly seems to have been a principle, for it has been repeated in Deuteronomy 21:3.

Concerning John 18:37, I very much appreciate McGarvey and Pendleton's comments about this exchange from *The Fourfold Gospel*:

> Jesus admits that he is a king, but asks a question which forms the strongest negation that he is a king in the sense contained in the Jewish accusation. Had he been a king in that sense, Pilate would have been the one most likely to know it. The question also, by an indirect query as to the accuser, reveals to Pilate's mind that no Roman had accused him. He was accused of the Jews, and when had that restless, rebellious people ever found fault with a man who sought to free them from the galling Roman yoke? The strong practical mind of the Roman at once caught the drift of Christ's questions, and perceived that the title, "King of the Jews" had in it a double meaning, so that it might be construed in some unpolitical sense. What this sense was he could not tell, for he was not a Jew. The mysteries of that nation were of no interest to him save where his office compelled him to understand them. Pilate concedes that the accusation against Jesus comes from an unexpected and suspicious source, and he asks Jesus to tell him plainly by what means he had incurred the enmity of the leaders of His people.

There are so many other places to which we could have turned to demonstrate the fulfillment of the kingly prophecies in Jesus. We could have gone to Peter's discourse on the Day of Pentecost in Acts 2, particularly verses 30-35, to demonstrate the kingship of Jesus. The statement made by the angel Gabriel to Mary in Luke 1:32-33 is yet another passage that accomplishes the same thing. I chose John 18:37 because of the clear statement of Jesus to Pilate, and Matthew 21:5 because Scripture is the only infallible interpreter of prophecy, and it is a quote from Zechariah 9:9. There application is made to Jesus – the King.

4. Judge – Isaiah 33:22

> For the Lord is our judge, the Lord is our lawgiver, the Lord is our king; He will save us (Isa. 33:22).

The Messianic nature of this prophecy simply cannot be denied. Because of the trilogy of offices mentioned in it, all related and finding embodiment in one being, it can refer to none other. Jamieson, Fausett, and Brown, in *Commentary on the Whole Bible*, put it succinctly, "Judge . . . lawgiver . . . king – perfect ideal of the theocracy, to be realized under Messiah alone; the judicial, legislative, and administrative functions as king to be exercised by Him in person" (549).

Fulfillment – John 12:47-48; 2 Timothy 4:1

> If anyone hears My sayings and does not keep them, I do not judge him; for I did not come to judge the world, but to save the world. He who rejects Me and does not receive My sayings, has one who judges him; the word I spoke is what will judge him at the last day (John 12:47-48).

> I solemnly charge you in the presence of God and Christ Jesus, who is to judge the living and the dead and by His appearing and His kingdom (2 Tim. 4:1).

To reject the teaching of Jesus is to reject God. His words act as our judge, now and at His return. Our response to His teaching during our lives will determine what sentence will be pronounced when He comes back. Paul wrote in 2 Corinthians 5:10, "For we must all appear before the judgment seat of Christ, so that each one may be recompensed for his deeds in the body, according to what he has done, whether good or bad."

5. Anointed of the Holy Spirit – Isaiah 11:2

The Spirit of the Lord will rest on Him, the spirit of wisdom and understanding, the spirit of counsel and strength, the spirit of knowledge and the fear of the Lord (Isa. 11:2).

Contextually, this is a very interesting prophecy. At the close of Isaiah 10, Isaiah had foretold of the humbling of the mighty Assyrians. Now, in contrast to the humbling of the mighty, in chapter 11 he tells of the exaltation of the lowly. Out of the family of Jesse, out of the house of David, which had fallen into humble circumstances, would come forth a branch. This branch would be the Messiah.

Verse 2 of Isaiah 11 indicates that the Spirit would dwell with Him, that He would be abundantly endowed with the Holy Spirit. In *Christology of the Old Testament*, Hengstenberg writes:

> Perhaps the circumstance, that the Messiah is first said to be endowed with the Spirit of God in general terms, and that then particular gifts are mentioned by way of example, indicates that he would not, like all other servants of God, be endowed with any merely particular gifts. Although the word "rests" is elsewhere spoken of the Spirit of God, when it takes possession of the mind, yet here it seems to be particularly emphatic. The Prophets were powerfully seized by the Spirit, and then again deserted; but His influence with the Messiah shall be uniform and permanent (188).

Fulfillment – Matthew 3:16-17; Luke 4:17-21

After being baptized, Jesus came up immediately from the water; and behold, the heavens were opened, and He saw the Spirit of God descending as a dove and lighting on Him, and behold, a voice out of the heavens said, "This is my beloved Son in whom I am well pleased" (Matt. 3:16-17).

And the book of the prophet Isaiah was handed to Him. And He opened the book and found the place where it was written, "The Spirit of the Lord is upon Me, because He anointed Me to preach the gospel to the poor. He has sent Me to proclaim release to the captives, and recovery of sight to the blind, to set free those who are oppressed, to proclaim the favorable year of the Lord." And He closed the book, gave it back to the attendant and sat down; and the eyes of all in the synagogue were fixed on Him. And He began to say to them, "Today this Scripture has been fulfilled in your hearing" (Luke 4:17-21).

Verse 2 of Isaiah 11 indicated that the Spirit of God would dwell with Him and that He would be endowed with the Holy Spirit without measure. When the Holy Spirit descended upon Jesus, and John would later testify, "I have seen the Spirit descending as a dove out of heaven, and He remained upon Him" (John 1:32), our Lord received the promised anointing of the Spirit. Many are of the opinion that the fact that the Spirit was "upon" Him signifies the permanent abiding anointing of the Christ.

Of this event, *The Pulpit Commentary* states, "God the Father consecrated his incarnate Son by this Divine anointing. Now he was revealed as the Priest forever after the order of Melchizedek; the King to whom the Lord God would give the throne of his father David; the Prophet who would declare to the faithful all that we need to know, all that we can know while we are in the flesh, of that God whom no man hath seen at any time" (XV, #81).

We should also mention that the message from heaven shows that God recognized Jesus as His only begotten Son and expressed His pleasure in Him. Additionally, the context indicates that there was a multitude present at the time of the baptism. Did they hear the voice and see the dove? I don't believe that the multitude saw or heard, for that would have been a very early announcement of the Messiahship of Jesus; and our Lord would often say, on later occasions, that His time had not yet come. John and Jesus saw, heard, and understood, but I believe much more would have been made of this if the gathered crowd had also seen and heard.

The event found in Luke 4:17-21 took place at Nazareth, the hometown of Jesus, which was an obscure village of less than desirable reputation. As was the Lord's custom, He went into the synagogue of wherever He was on the Sabbath day. Standing to read, He was delivered the book of the prophet Isaiah. The passage that He chose was Isaiah 61:1-2.

Some may wonder why Jesus went back to this small town. He

could have labored exclusively in the large centers of commerce and population. Why go to such a small and insignificant place, even if it was His hometown? I believe the answer to that question lies in the text He chose to read. The gospel is not just for the rich, the best educated, or those with the most desirable reputations. It is for all. So, in this little village of Nazareth, in its one synagogue, where it had been Jesus' custom during His youth to attend, He revealed Himself to those among whom He had grown up. Of all the prophetic passages that Jesus could have chosen, He chose one that presented the Messiah as endowed with the Holy Spirit, a minister to the sick and afflicted, a teacher of the neglected, a Savior, and comforter of the oppressed. With all of the eyes of the people in the synagogue fastened upon Him, Jesus said, "Today this Scripture has been fulfilled in your hearing." It was the same as saying, "He that is speaking to you is the Promised One."

6. Galilee – Isaiah 9:1-2

But there will be no more gloom for her who was in anguish; in earlier times He treated the land of Zebulun and the land of Naphtali with contempt, but later on He shall make it glorious, by the way of the sea, on the other side of Jordan, Galilee of the Gentiles. The people who walk in darkness will see a great light; those who live in a dark land, the light will shine on them (Isa. 9:1-2).

Galilee of the Nations, or Galilee of the Gentiles, was the region chiefly held by the tribes of Zebulun and Naphtali. This area constituted the border for a number of heathen nations. Not only were there many Gentiles living in the vicinity of Galilee, many lived in the region itself. It would appear that the less than favorable view that many held of Galilee, evidenced by Nathanael's statement in John 1:46, and the questions of the Jews in John 7:41 and 52, were primarily a result of the mingling of the inhabitants of Galilee with the Gentiles.

However, there was a glory and an honor to be had for this region, for a magnificent light would shine among them. This occurred when Jesus fixed His residence in Capernaum and spent a major part of His ministry in the land of Galilee. Again, from *Christology of the Old Testament*, we find:

Christ passed the greatest part of the time of His public ministry in Galilee; there lay Capernaum, His ordinary place of abode; in Galilee were most of His disciples; there He performed many miracles; there the preaching of the gospel met with much success. . . .Altogether similar is the passage in the first verse of the fifth chapter of Micah. . . . As there, the birth of the Messiah shall confer honour upon the hitherto obscure Bethlehem, so here shall Galilee, hitherto held in contempt, upon which the Jews cast the reproach that no prophet arose there, be raised to honour and rendered illustrious by the manifestation of the Messiah (174).

Fulfillment – Matthew 4:12-16

Now when Jesus heard that John had been taken into custody, He withdrew into Galilee; and leaving Nazareth, He came and settled in Capernaum, which is by the sea, in the region of Zebulun and Naphtali. This was to fulfill what was spoken through Isaiah the prophet: "The land of Zebulun and the land of Naphtali, by the way of the sea, beyond the Jordan, Galilee of the Gentiles – The people who were sitting in darkness saw a great light, and those who were sitting in the land and shadow of death, upon them a light dawned" (Matt. 4:12-16).

After learning of John's arrest, Jesus left Judea for Galilee. In Galilee, He made His base of operations the city of Capernaum. There is no need to wonder as to what the prophecy of Isaiah 9:1-2 referred. Matthew infallibly tells us. We see Jesus, filled with the Holy Spirit, going to Galilee in fulfillment of prophecy. It was time for Him to manifest Himself more fully.

One thing we can wonder about is how those claiming to be believers can continue to deny clear statements of Scripture. A case in point involves William Barclay, who repeatedly makes statements such as the following in his *Daily Study Bible Series*, concerning Matthew 4:12-17: "It was Matthew's habit to find in the Old Testament something which he could use as a prophecy about every event in Jesus' life. He finds such a prophecy in Isaiah 9:1-2. In fact, that is another of the prophecies which Matthew tears violently from its context in his own extraordinary way" (I: 75). While it shouldn't by now, such audacity of man always takes me by surprise.

7. Worker of Miracles – Isaiah 35:5-6

Then the eyes of the blind will be opened and the ears of the deaf will be unstopped. Then the lame will leap like a deer, and the tongue of the mute will shout for joy. For waters will break forth in the wilderness and streams in the Arabah (Isa. 35:5-6).

Contextually, chapters 34 and 35 of Isaiah tell of the judgment of the enemies against God's people, most specifically the Assyrians and then the Babylonians, and the resultant joy among God's children. The language of Isaiah 35:5-6 figuratively describes that great joy that God's people would feel. However, it speaks of that anti-typical time of the Messiah and the miracles that He would perform.

Fulfillment – Matthew 11:2-5

Now when John, while imprisoned, heard of the works of Christ, he sent word by his disciples and said to Him, "Are you the Expected One, or shall we look for someone else?" Jesus answered and said to them, "Go and report to John what you hear and see: the blind receive sight and the lame walk, the lepers are cleansed and the deaf hear, the dead are raised up, and the poor have the gospel preached to them. And blessed is he who does not take offense at Me" (Matt. 11:2-5).

The Lord's answer clearly indicates that it was acknowledged that when the Messiah came, He would be accompanied by miracles. These signs and wonders were offered as significant proof that He was the Christ, the Anointed One. His answer demonstrates the Messianic nature of Isaiah 35:5-6, as well as its fulfillment.

"Are you the Expected One, or shall we look for someone else?" Was this a question for the benefit of the one who had first recognized and pointed out the Lamb of God? Was this for the benefit of the one who had seen heaven open and the Spirit descending upon the head of Jesus like a dove? I am inclined to believe that it was. Many have suggested that this message was intended merely to satisfy the doubts of the followers of John. Others contend that his question really meant, "Are you truly the Jesus to whom I bore my testimony?" Still others say it implies no real doubt on John's part, but that it was meant only as a push, an attempt to get Jesus to change His approach and to strongly manifest Himself as the Messiah of the nation. Others yet find in John's question a gentle rebuke of Jesus for allowing John to languish in prison when a simple statement of Jesus was sufficient to miraculously tear down the walls that held him. All of these suggestions, while worthy of consideration, seem to be meant to save the reputation of John, as if to say that there was no possible way for John to have had any doubt. I do not believe that to be true or necessary.

John had been in prison for some time. This would have been a very trying situation for a man of the wilderness, accustomed to a free and open life. Being confined with no work, with no release for his considerable energies, very probably affected the spirit that had been so strong. Perhaps John found himself sinking into melancholy like his prototype, Elijah. It may very well have been so. John was a man of strength, very bold and courageous – but let us not forget that he was a man, subject to weaknesses and inconsistencies. No man lives at his highest level at all times, and the Bible is very clear that even great men of God sometimes fail, and sometimes they fail in what had appeared to be their strongest attribute. For example, Elijah failed in courage, Moses in meekness, and Peter in steadfastness. Perhaps John was a case in point. He had waited for a long time, locked in prison. Why should we be surprised if he had become impatient and despairing? Surely John had heard reports of the actions, works, and teachings of Jesus. They were so holy, and yet in some respects so unlike his own. No wonder he was perplexed.

The Bible consistently presents men as they really were. It does not paint idealized pictures. It shows the imperfections as well as the good. I find it encouraging that, in the Scriptures, we see real men, truly great men of God, men who fought the good fight and won the race, yet they failed from time to time. They wavered sometimes, doubted at others, but came out triumphant. In his troubled state, John sent directly to Jesus.

With kindness and gentleness Jesus responded to the two disciples of John. "Go and report to John what you hear and see." What was it that they had seen and heard? The blind received their sight, the lame walked, the lepers were cleansed, the deaf heard, the dead were raised, and the poor were having the gospel preached to them. This was substantially a quote of Isaiah 35:5-6. While I did not quote it, included in Jesus' response was a word of encouragement to John, "Blessed is he who does not take offense at Me." In other words, "John, don't find me a stumbling block to your faith. Remain strong and believe."

8. Teacher of Parables – Psalm 78:2

I will open my mouth in a parable; I will utter dark sayings of old (Psa. 78:2).

Psalm 78 is called a "Maskil of Asaph." A *maskil* was a song written to teach and edify. Asaph, about whom we can read in 1 Chronicles 6:31-33, 39; 15:9; 16:5; and 2 Chronicles 29:30, was a singer and a cymbal player, as well as a seer and inspired writer of several psalms. He writes in Psalm 78:2, "I will open my mouth in a parable." This form of teaching, speaking in parables as used by Asaph, was typical of what One much greater than Asaph would do. The Lord, the Master Teacher, would use nature or human circumstances to teach great spiritual lessons.

Fulfillment – Matthew 13:34-35

All these things Jesus spoke to the crowds in parables, and He did not speak to them without a parable. This was to fulfill what was spoken through the prophet: "I will open my mouth in parables; I will utter things hidden since the foundation of the world" (Matt. 13:34-35).

Here is a divinely inspired interpretation of Psalm 78:2. It referred to the Messiah ultimately and was fulfilled in Jesus.

The reference to Psalm 78:2 appears to have a threefold meaning. First, no teacher compares in history to Jesus in the use of parables. What about the second clause of that quotation? The following quote is from *The Pulpit Commentary*:

Truths never before revealed have now been revealed by Christ's parables, especially by those two which have just been related. For in these it has been affirmed that outsiders, i.e., those belonging to other nations than the Jewish nation, shall seek the protection of the kingdom of heaven, and also that the whole world, including, therefore, these Gentile nations, shall become permeated with its principles. It may well be though that the clause refers to the announcement of these great truths. But this interpretation, however, if taken alone, is not enough. For the evangelist is not speaking of Christ revealing truths to men generally. On the contrary, he says that Christ does not reveal them to the multitudes (v. 10) a contrast which the emphatic language of v. 34 would probably suggest, even though it is not expressly mentioned. It is, therefore, likely that it was this latter fact to which the evangelist specially wished to refer by his quotation of the second clause. Hence, to make his meaning clearer, he has modified its language. As he quotes it, not merely "enigmatical sayings," but "things hidden" (and that from the foundation of the world) are uttered by Christ; but these are now no longer "hidden" to those to whom he speaks them. This complete meaning of the clause – revelation to his disciples of truths before hidden – corresponds to the idea in v. 11 (XV: 10).

9. Light to the Gentiles – Isaiah 49:6

He says, "It is too small a thing that You should be My Servant to raise up the tribes of Jacob and to restore the preserved ones of Israel; I will also make You a light of the nations so that My salvation may reach to the end of the earth" (Isa. 49:6).

In the several chapters preceding chapter 49, glorious and wonderful things have been said concerning the deliverance of the Jews out of Babylonian captivity. Indeed, as typical of the Messiah, Cyrus has been named as the anointed of God who would bring this deliverance about. While many of the predicted blessings have a more immediate reference to the delivery from captivity, they have a further intention and higher fulfillment in another delivery – the delivery of the world from the bondage of sin by the Messiah.

Of Isaiah 49:6, Jamieson, Fausset, and Brown write in their *Commentary on the Whole Bible*, "It is not enough honor for Thee (the Messiah – g.l.) to raise up Jacob and Israel, but I design for Thee more, viz., that Thou shouldest be the means of enlightening the Gentiles" (572).

Fulfillment – Acts 13:45-47

But when the Jews saw the crowds, they were filled with jealousy and began contradicting the things spoken by Paul, and were blaspheming. Paul and Barnabas spoke out boldly and said, "It was necessary that the word of God be spoken to you first; since you repudiate it and judge yourselves unworthy of eternal life, behold, we are turning to the Gentiles. For so the Lord has commanded us, 'I have placed You as a light for the Gentiles, that You may bring salvation to the end of the earth'" (Acts. 13:45-47).

In Antioch of Pisidia, Paul and Barnabas, in a magnificent presentation, demonstrated that Jesus was the fulfillment of that to which the Law and the Prophets are pointed. When certain of the Jews saw the great multitude that assembled the next Sabbath day, nearly the whole city, they began contradicting and blaspheming the truth that had been spoken by Paul. Paul and Barnabas quoted Isaiah 49:6 and applied it to their turning to the Gentiles. As prophesied, the glorious light of the gospel was presented first to the Jews – those of Jacob and Israel – and then permitted to shine among the Gentiles.

Chapter Five

Prophecies Concerning His Character

No person who has walked the hills and valleys of earth has ever possessed perfect moral character; no one except Jesus. Presented in the pages of the gospels is the picture of sinless perfection, perfect moral character, embodied in our Lord. Truly, nothing else could have been the case as far as the Son of God, the Savior of the world, was concerned.

The International Standard Bible Encyclopedia states:

His is the one life in humanity in which is presented a perfect knowledge and unbroken fellowship with the Father, undeviating obedience to His will, answering devotion unto the severest strain of temptation and suffering to the highest ideal of goodness. The ethical ideal was never raised to so absolute a height as it is in the teaching of Jesus, and the miracle is that, high as it is in its unsullied purity, the character of Jesus corresponds with it, and realizes it. Word and life for once in history perfectly agree (III: 1630).

The three prophesies that I have chosen to examine in this chapter deal with specific incidents in the life of the Messiah. Each one of these events serves as a marvelous demonstration of the moral character of our Lord. Oh, that we could be more like Him everyday.

1. Zeal – Psalm 69:9

For zeal for Your house has consumed me, and the reproaches of those who reproach You have fallen on me (Psa. 69:9).

What David had in mind as he wrote these words cannot be definitively stated. Perhaps the indignities done to God's name and the lack of respect and reverence for His tabernacle caused David to be "consumed" by his zeal for God. One thing is certain, however. Through David the Holy Spirit was prophesying that this same consuming zeal for God would be found in Jesus. In his booklet, *Messianic Prophecy*, Hugo McCord wrote, "The second part of Psalm 69:9, 'and the reproaches of them that reproach thee are fallen upon me,' indicates that David, in defending the tabernacle, was himself defamed by evil men who were desecrating the sacred tabernacle. Whatever the local situation that called forth David's utterance, the second part of Psalm 69:9 was also a prediction of what would happen to Jesus" (15-16).

Fulfillment – John 2:13-17

The Passover of the Jews was near, and Jesus went up to Jerusalem. He found in the temple those who were selling oxen, sheep, and doves, and the moneychangers seated at their tables. He made a scourge of cords, and drove them all out of the temple, with the sheep and the oxen; and He poured out the coins of the money changers and overturned their tables; and to those who were selling the doves He said, "Take these things away; stop making My Father's house a place of business." His disciples remembered that it was written, "Zeal for Your house will consume Me" (John 2:13-17).

The first cleansing of the temple took place at the Passover Feast, the first of the four such feasts that Jesus would observe during His public ministry. It was one of the three great annual feasts of the Jews. Vast crowds would flock to the city of Jerusalem for its observance and the temple would be the focal point of activity. To give an idea of the crowds involved, Josephus estimated that in one year 256,500 lambs were slaughtered for Passover in Jerusalem and there were ten men present for every lamb. That means 2,565,000 men were present in Jerusalem for the feast. Even taking into account Josephus' proclivity for exaggeration, that is a tremendous number of people. The streets would have been thronged with the multitudes moving toward the temple, and further crowded by the merchants selling sheep, oxen, and doves, as well as the tables of the moneychangers.

Why were the moneychangers necessary? Because of a law established in Exodus 30:11-16:

> The Lord also spoke to Moses, saying, "When you take a census of the sons of Israel to number them, then each one of them shall give a ransom for himself to the Lord, when you number them, so that there will be no plague among them, when you number them. This is what everyone who is numbered shall give: half a shekel according to the shekel of the sanctuary (the shekel is twenty gerahs), half a shekel as a contribution to the Lord. Everyone who is numbered, from twenty years old and over, shall give the contribution to the Lord. The rich shall not pay more and the poor shall not pay less than the half shekel, when you give the contribution to the Lord, to make atonement for yourselves. You shall take the atonement money from the sons of Israel and shall give it for the service of the tent of meeting, that it may be a memorial for the sons of Israel before the Lord, to make atonement for yourselves."

Twenty days before the Passover the priests began to collect this half shekel paid yearly by every adult Israelite, rich or poor, as atonement money for his soul and to be applied to the expenses of the tabernacle (or temple) service. All different kinds of money were in circulation at that time from many different countries and governments, and some of it was defiled with heathen symbols and inscriptions. It was not lawful to pay with this kind of money, and each was obliged to pay with a little silver coin. Therefore, an individual would go to the moneychangers to receive this coin in exchange for his own currency, and would generally be charged 5% interest on the exchange.

All of this merchandising would have been excusable as necessary if it had been confined to the streets leading to the temple. It had not been so confined. The considerable space of the Court of the Gentiles had been used by the merchants and moneychangers, with the approval of the Sadducees, as their marketplace.

Frederick Farrar gives this vivid description of the scene in *The Life of Christ*:

> There, in the actual Court of the Gentiles, steaming with heat in

the burning April day, and filling the Temple with stench and filth, were penned whole flocks of sheep and oxen, while the drivers and pilgrims stood bartering and bargaining around them. There were the men with their great wicker cages filled with doves, and under the shadow of the arcades, formed by quadruple rows of Corinthian columns, sat the moneychangers with their tables covered with piles of various small coins, while, as they reckoned and wrangled in the most dishonest of trades, their greedy eyes twinkled with the lust of gain. And this was the entrance court to the Temple of the Most High! The court which was a witness that that house should be a House of Prayer for all nations had been degraded into a place, which for foulness, was more like a shambles, and for bustling commerce, more like a densely-crowded bazaar; while the lowing of oxen, the bleating of sheep, the Babel of many languages, and huckstering and wrangling, and clinking of money and of balances (perhaps not always just), might be heard in the adjoining courts, disturbing the chant of the Levites and the prayers of the priests! (159)

Filled with righteous indignation at this abuse of His Father's house, Jesus fashioned a whip out of several small cords and unleashed His divine wrath upon those who prostituted God's house. He drove out the sheep and the oxen and those who tended them. Then He turned His attention to the tables of the moneychangers and turned them over, spilling their coins onto the floor of the Court of the Gentiles. He told those who sold doves to remove them from the temple and with divine authority and justification He said, "Make not my Father's house a house of merchandise." Seeing His righteous indignation, His disciples found their minds drawn back to Psalm 69:9, where David had written, "For zeal for Your house has consumed me, and the reproaches of those who reproach You have fallen on me." Three years later this same scene would be repeated at the beginning of Jesus' final week.

2. Enters Jerusalem on a Donkey – Zechariah 9:9

Rejoice greatly, O daughter of Zion! Shout in triumph, O daughter of Jerusalem! Behold, your king is coming to you; He is just and endowed with salvation, humble, and mounted on a donkey, even on a colt, the foal of a donkey (Zech. 9:9).

We examined this prophecy in the previous chapter. Our emphasis there was on the fact that the Promised One was to be a king. I included it in this chapter because of what it tells us about the character of the king and the nature of His earthly reign.

Physical, earthly kings placed great importance upon pomp and ceremony. They rode on regal horses with a great display of their power, wealth, and prominence. The Messiah would be different. His reign would not be characterized by worldly splendor but by humility. His entrance into His city would not be accompanied by pomp and ceremony but by the trappings of lowliness. This king would be unique.

Fulfillment – Matthew 21:1-7

When they had approached Jerusalem and had come to Bethphage, at the Mount of Olives, then Jesus sent two disciples, saying to them, "Go into the village opposite you, and immediately you will find a donkey tied there and a colt with her; untie them and bring them to Me. If anyone says anything to you, you shall say, 'The Lord has need of them,' and immediately he will send them.'" This took place to fulfill what was spoken through the prophet: "Say to the daughter of Zion, 'Behold your king is coming to you, gentle, and mounted on a donkey, even on a colt, the foal of a beast of burden.'" The disciples went and did just as Jesus had instructed them, and brought the donkey and the colt, and laid their coats on them; and He sat on the coats (Matt. 21:1-7).

Having secured the animals in exactly the manner that Jesus had said they would, the disciples brought them to Jesus. Evidently they did not know which animal Jesus would choose to ride, for they put their garments on both of them. This provided a place to sit and was also a sign of honor (2 Kings 9:13). These garments would have been the cloak, worn over the tunics or shirts.

Of this wonderful display of humility on the part of Jesus, Matthew Henry in his *Commentary in One Volume*, wrote:

When he made his public entry into his own city (and it was the only passage of his life that had anything in it magnificent in the eye of the world), he chose to ride, not upon a stately horse, or in a chariot, as great men used to ride, but upon an ass, nor was it an ass fitted for use, but an ass's colt, a little foolish, unmanageable thing, likely to displace his rider. He had no saddle, no trappings, no equipage, but his disciples' clothes thrown upon the colt; for he made of himself no reputation when he visited us in great humility (1185).

3. He Would Make Intercession for His Persecutors –Isaiah 53:12

Therefore, I will allot Him a portion with the great, and He will divide the booty with the strong; because He poured out Himself to death, and was numbered with the transgressors, yet He Himself bore the sin of many, and interceded for the transgressors (Isa. 53:12).

This prophecy could have been included in a later chapter dealing with the death of the Lord. But I chose to include it here because of what it reveals to us about the character of Jesus. While the intercession referred to is not limited to the prayers of our Lord, but rather encompasses His vicarious death and suffering as well, it does indicate His love and compassion for lost souls.

From *Commentary in One Volume*, Matthew Henry wrote of Isaiah 53:12:

In His sufferings He made intercession for the transgressors, for those that reviled and crucified him; He prayed, "Father forgive them," thereby showing, not only that He forgave them, but that He was now doing that upon which their forgiveness, and the forgiveness of all other transgressors, were to be founded. That prayer was the language of His blood, crying not for vengeance, but for mercy (908).

Fulfillment – Luke 23:34

But Jesus was saying, "Father, forgive them; for they do not know what they are doing." And they cast lots, dividing His garments among themselves (Luke 23:34).

Jesus taught His followers to love their enemies and to pray for those that despitefully use them and persecute them. Could He have exemplified His teaching any more than He did with this statement from the cross?

In *The Pulpit Commentary* we find:

Conscious, not only of perfect innocence, but of the purest and even the loftiest aims, Jesus Christ found himself not only unrewarded and unappreciated, but misunderstood, ill treated, condemned on a totally false charge, sentenced to the most cruel and shameful death a man could die. What wonder if, under those conditions, all the kindliness of his nature had turned to sourness of spirit! At this very moment he was the object of the most heartless cruelty man could inflict, and must have been suffering pain of body and of mind that was literally agonizing. At such a time, and under such treatment, he forgets himself to remember the guilt of those who were so shamefully wronging him. Instead of entertaining any feeling of resentment, he desired that they might be forgiven their wrong-doing. He did not haughtily and contemptuously decline to condemn them; he did not hardly and reluctantly forgive them; he found for them a generous extenuation; he sincerely prayed his heavenly Father to forgive them. Human magnanimity could hardly go further than that (XVI, Luke: 254).

Jan 12

Chapter Six

Prophecies Concerning His Betrayal

Thus far we have been blessed to see a gloriously detailed picture presented in the Old Testament of the Anointed One, the Christ who was to come. We have read of the circumstances of His birth and we have noted the specifics of His lineage. The type and nature of His ministry have been examined in the prophecies, as well as through various aspects of His character.

Now we will notice darker events that were to happen. Not all was to be glorious when viewed from an earthly perspective. The Promised One would experience many trials and much sorrow.

1. Betrayed By a Friend – Psalm 41:9

Even my close friend in whom I trusted, who ate my bread, has lifted up his heel against me (Psa. 41:9).

This psalm brings to mind Ahithophel, a man about whom we read in 2 Samuel 15:12. We are told there that he was David's counselor, making him a respected man, one whose advice was sought by David. In 2 Samuel 16:23 we read, "The advice of Ahithophel, which he gave in those days, was as if one inquired of the word of God; so was all the advice of Ahithophel regarded by both David and Absalom."

Yet this confidante, this personal advisor to King David, betrayed David and threw his allegiance to the rebellious son of the king, Absalom. Psalm 41 expresses the feelings of the betrayed king. In the east, to eat bread with someone was a sign of friendship and loyalty. In this sad case, that friendship was betrayed and the loyalty was a fleeting thing.

Fulfillment – John 13:18, 26-27

I do not speak of all of you. I know the ones I have chosen; but it is that the Scripture may be fulfilled, "He who eats my bread has lifted up his heel against me" (John 13:18).

Jesus then answered, "That is the one for whom I shall dip the morsel and give it to him." So when He had dipped the morsel, He took and gave it to Judas, the son of Simon Iscariot. After the morsel, Satan then entered into him. Therefore Jesus said to him, "What you do, do quickly" (John 13:26-27).

As David was betrayed by Ahithophel, so was Jesus betrayed by Judas. In typical fashion, one betrayed an earthly king, the other a heavenly king, Jesus Christ the Lord. Thus Psalm 41:9 was fulfilled.

John 13 is not the only chapter that describes what was taking place at the time. Matthew 26:21-25, Mark 14:18-21, and Luke 22:21-23 all add something that helps us to understand the unfolding of this event. When Jesus told the apostles, "I do not speak of all of you. I know the ones I have chosen," obviously the disciples were amazed at the news and wanted to know who would do such a thing. When they asked, "Is it I, Lord?" the meaning is, "Surely it is not I." Jesus narrowed the possibilities by saying, "It is one of the twelve, one who dips with Me in the bowl" (Mark 14:20). At such a gathering there would have been two or three bowls into which they would dip their bread. So it would have been one of those sitting closest to Jesus. John, the disciple whom Jesus loved, was sitting the closest to the Lord, and Peter encouraged John to find out who it was. When John asked, "Lord, who is it?" Jesus said, "That is the one for whom I shall dip the morsel, and give it to him." Jesus then dipped the morsel and gave it to Judas. So it went from twelve, to three or four, to one – Judas. This seems only to have hardened Judas. His question, "Is it I?" wasn't to repent but only to continue the deception. As the language seems to indicate, Judas' doing that was in some way the final giving of himself over to Satan. Note now, Jesus did not command the deed, but since it had already been decided upon by Judas, Jesus dismissed him with the words, "What you do, do quickly." Judas had refused all appeals. It was time to do what he had decided to do.

Understand that Jesus was following a path that He had come to follow – this was why He came to earth. But Judas did not have to do what he did. Don't apologize for Judas. He had a choice and he made it. There is a certain pathos in "and it was night" (John 13:30). The light of day had faded for Judas. Because of what he was doing and would do, only night and doom remained.

2. Sold for Thirty Pieces of Silver – Zechariah 11:12

I said to them, "If it is good in your sight, give me my wages; but if not, never mind!" So they weighed out thirty shekels of silver as my wages (Zech. 11:12).

An appreciation of this prophecy, as well as others that will be examined, requires a few preliminary words about the book of Zechariah in general. The book is decidedly Messianic, comparing favorably with Isaiah in that regard. It contains a great deal of apocalyptic symbolism. In *A Commentary on the Minor Prophets*, Homer Hailey tells us this about the book:

The Messiah is presented as "the Branch" or "Sprout" of David, a servant of Jehovah. He comes as a king, lowly in spirit, providing salvation for the people. He comes as a shepherd rejected, sold for the price of a wounded slave, and finally pierced for the sheep who would then be scattered. But he redeems a remnant, and through him the divine sovereignty of Jehovah is restored. The kingdom will be one of glory, with everything pertaining to it consecrated to the Lord (319).

Zechariah 11:12 tells of the estimate of the value of the work of the shepherd, the Messiah, by the people. According to Exodus 21:32, thirty pieces of silver was the price the owner of an ox was to pay if the animal gored someone's servant. So the people's estimation of the value of the work of the shepherd was a sign of contempt – thirty pieces of silver, the price of an injured slave.

Fulfillment – Matthew 26:14-15

Then one of the twelve, named Judas Iscariot, went to the chief priests
and said, "What are you willing to give me to betray him to you?"
And they weighed out thirty pieces of silver to him (Matt. 26:14-
15).

Judas went to the chief priests offering to deliver Jesus up to them.
Just what prompted Judas, what motivated him to do what he did,
the Bible does not say a great deal about. Luke states that Satan
entered into him (Luke 22:3). The emphasis on money, the thirty
pieces of silver, certainly indicates greed. You might remember Judas'
anger when Mary anointed Jesus in John 12. It wasn't concern for
the poor that prompted his anger; it was his greed. So avarice was
certainly part of his character. John also mentions in 13:2 the devil's
part in this act. It should be made clear that Judas was not a subject
of demonic possession that he could not resist. Judas opened the
door, and the devil came in. He deliberately yielded to temptation.

The chief priests paid Judas his thirty pieces of silver in advance to
seal the bargain, and from that moment on he looked for an opportunity to do his deed – to deliver Jesus to the chief priests at a time
when He was away from the crowd.

The Pulpit Commentary says:

Christ had taken upon him the form of a bond-servant, and here was
reckoned as such. The transaction had been typically shadowed forth
when another Judas sold his brother for twenty pieces of silver; when
Ahithophel gave counsel against David, his familiar friend; and when
Zechariah wrote, "I said unto them, 'If ye think good, give me my
price; and if not, forbear.' So they weighed for my price thirty pieces
of silver" (XV: 518).

3. Money Thrown in God's House – Zech. 11:13
4. Price for Potter's Field – Zech. 11:13

Then the Lord said to me, "Throw it to the potter, that magnificent
price at which I was valued by them." So I took the thirty shekels of
silver and threw them to the potter in the house of the Lord (Zech.
11:13).

We will examine both of these prophecies together. In verse 12 of Zechariah 11, the value of the work of the shepherd (the Messiah) had been placed by the people at the paltry sum of thirty pieces of silver, the price of an injured slave. Jehovah's contempt for their estimation is clear. Hailey wrote, "The casting away of the paltry price at which Jehovah had been prized was done publicly, before the Lord, that both He and the people could be witness to the insult thrust on Him and that He could bring them to account for their deed." This evidence of rejection and ingratitude, thirty pieces of silver, was cast away before the Lord and, being blood money, used to purchase a potter's field wherein to bury strangers.

Fulfillment – Matthew 27:3-10

Then when Judas, who had betrayed Him, saw that He had been condemned, he felt remorse and returned the thirty pieces of silver to the chief priests and elders, saying, "I have sinned by betraying innocent blood." But they said, "What is that to us? See to that yourself." And he threw the pieces of silver into the temple sanctuary and departed; and he went away and hanged himself. The chief priests took the pieces of silver and said, "It is not lawful to put them into the temple treasury, since it is the price of blood." And they conferred together and with the money bought the Potter's Field as a burial place for strangers. For this reason that field has been called the Field of Blood to this day. Then that which was spoken through Jeremiah the prophet was fulfilled: "And they took the thirty pieces of silver, the price of the one whose price had been set by the sons of Israel; and they gave them for the Potter's Field, as the Lord directed me" (Matt. 27:3-10).

In the gospel according to Matthew, Judas' remorse and suicide follow the condemnation by the Sanhedrin, but precede the condemnation by Pilate. We are going to approach it that way, but the actual order of events was probably a little different. It is probable that Judas' remorse and suicide followed the final condemnation by Pilate. *The Fourfold Gospel* says, "The incident is introduced in advance of its chronological order so as not to interrupt the subsequent narration."

Seeing Jesus condemned to death, Judas felt the awful weight of what he had done. He had betrayed "innocent blood." There is an important point that needs to be made concerning the statement in Matthew 27:3 that Judas "repented himself." McGarvey and Pendleton wrote:

> There are two Greek words which are translated "repented," the one properly translated, *metanoeo*, which means literally "to know after" and which therefore means a change of mind or purpose; and the other, *metamellomai*, which is used here and which means literally "to care after," indicates a sorrow for the past. The first should be translated "repent," the second, "regret." Trench draws the distinction thus: "He who had *changed his mind* about the past is the way to change everything; he who has an *after care* may have little or nothing more than a selfish dread of the consequences of what he had done." Considering the prophecy which had been uttered with regard to Judas' act (Matt. 26:24), he had good reason to fear the consequences. While he testifies as to the innocence of Jesus, he expresses affection for him (*The Fourfold Gospel*, 720).

Judas apparently found the priests in the sanctuary of the temple, indicating that he was standing right outside the Holy Place. I believe Judas cast the money because he feared the consequences of what he had done – not out of any true remorse for his sin against Jesus.

The reasoning of the priests concerning the use of the money was ridiculous. They were perfectly willing to take money out of the treasury as payment for an unholy and terrible deed, but they were not willing to take it back and put it again into the treasury because it had been so used – utter hypocrisy! The money was used to purchase "Potter's Field," a field devoid of use since it would have been stripped of its good soil for clay to be used in pottery. This then was a place for strangers to be buried because Gentiles were not permitted in Jewish graveyards. Hence, this field was called the "Field of Blood."

There are those who understand Acts 1:18-19 to indicate that this field was the same field where Judas hanged himself. Evidently Judas remained suspended for some days, and when the rope finally broke, or his neck gave way, he is said to have "fallen headlong" and that he "burst open in the middle and all his intestines gushed out." Thus, the reason, as given in Acts, for the field being known as the "Field of Blood."

Numerous questions have arisen, as well as a plethora of proposed answers, as to why Matthew ascribes this prophecy to Jeremiah. Some of the explanations offered have been: (1) A copyist simply transcribed the wrong name; (2) Zechariah was part of a roll headed by Jeremiah's work, the entire roll being referred to as Jeremiah; (3) Most plausibly to me, Matthew combined passages of Jeremiah, such as 18:2 and 19:1-2, with the statement in Zechariah and attributed the passage to the more noted prophet.

Chapter Seven

Prophecies Concerning His Suffering

Acts 17:1-3 reads, "Now when they had traveled through Amphipolis and Apollonia, they came to Thessalonica, where there was a synagogue of the Jews. And according to Paul's custom, he went to them, and for three Sabbaths reasoned with them from the Scriptures, explaining and giving evidence that the Christ had to suffer and rise again from the dead, and saying, 'This Jesus whom I am proclaiming to you is the Christ.'"

"Christ had to suffer." That is the subject of this chapter–the suffering of Christ. As did Paul, we will turn to the Old Testament and watch a truly remarkable picture unfold with accuracy and detail. It is the picture of the suffering Anointed One, the Messiah.

1. Forsaken By His Disciples – Zechariah 13:7

"Awake, O sword, against My Shepherd, and against the man, My Associate," declares the Lord of hosts. "Strike the Shepherd that the sheep may be scattered; and I will turn My hand against the little ones" (Zech. 13:7).

In the highly Messianic book of Zechariah, in addition to be presented as a "Branch" or "Sprout" of David, the Messiah is referred to as the Shepherd. Of Zechariah 13:7, Homer Hailey wrote in *A Commentary on the Minor Prophets*:

The Lord calls upon the sword to become active, to bestir itself. This does not mean that the shepherd was to be slain by the sword; the sword and smiting simply stands for his death through any instrument. The shepherd is "the good shepherd" who is willing to lay down His life for the sheep. "The man that is my fellow, saith Jehovah," indicates that though the shepherd is a man, He is "one united by community of nature" with Jehovah (Pusey). He is of the very essence of God and is identical in purpose with Him. The command "smite the shepherd," points out that which was done by "the determinate counsel and foreknowledge of God" (Acts 2:23). Upon the smiting of the shepherd the sheep were scattered (393).

Fulfillment – Matthew 26:31

Then Jesus said to them, "You will all fall away because of Me this night, for it is written, 'I will strike down the shepherd, and the sheep of the flock shall be scattered'" (Matt. 26:31).

Jesus makes application of the statement in Zechariah 13:7 to Himself and the scattering of His disciples. They would all be guilty of forsaking Him. As our Lord suffered through the events of the night and the subsequent crucifixion, He would be alone.

Albert Barnes makes an interesting comment concerning the words, "I will strike down the shepherd," in *Barnes' Notes on the New Testament*. He wrote:

This is the language of God the Father. I will smite, means either that I will give him up to be smitten, or that I will do it myself. Both of these things were done. God gave him up to the Jews and the Romans, to be smitten for the sins of the world (Romans 8:32), and he himself left him to deep and awful sorrows, to bear "the burden of the world's atonement" alone. See Mark 15:34 (128).

Truly the prophecy of Zechariah 13:7 finds its fulfillment in Jesus and in no other.

2. Accused By False Witnesses – Psalm 35:11

Malicious witnesses rise up; they ask me of things that I do not know (Psa. 35:11).

Psalm 35 is a psalm of David. It is an appeal to heaven prompted by malice and oppression against David by his enemies. Some believe that the internal evidence of the psalm indicates that it was written during the troublesome times David experienced with King Saul; others believe it was written during the days of unrest and revolt of David's older years. Either way, the actions of David's enemies toward him, including false accusations, were typical of what our Lord was to face.

From Matthew Henry's *Commentary in One Volume* we read, "False witnesses did rise up, who would swear anything; they laid to my charge things I knew not. This instance of the wrong done to David was typical, and had its accomplishment in the Son of David, against whom false witnesses did arise" (611).

Fulfillment – Matthew 26:59-61
Now the chief priests and the whole Council kept trying to obtain false testimony against Jesus, so that they might put Him to death. They did not find any, even though many false witnesses came forward. But later on two came forward and said, "This man stated, 'I am able to destroy the temple of God and to rebuild it in three days'" (Matt.26:59-61)

Just as David faced false accusations at the hands of his enemies, so too did Jesus. Many came, but why is special significance placed upon the last two? Because the Law of Moses forbade sentencing to death without the agreed testimony of two witnesses (Exod. 35:30). So deep was the hatred of the Jewish leaders for Jesus, and yet mindful of the need to present at least some semblance of legality, that they merely kept the false accusations coming until two agreed.

Reference was made to a statement that Jesus had uttered long before. It is found in John 2:19-22. At the time of that statement, the Lord's words were misunderstood as applying to Herod's temple. Now it appears that the Jewish rulers, hearing the Lord's prediction that He would rise from the dead after three days (Matt. 27:62-63), actually came to understand what Jesus had been talking about. In trying to build their case, the idea of tearing down the temple and rebuilding it in three days was a claim to deity, even though they knew at that time that Jesus had reference to His body and not the temple.

One of the most interesting aspects of the prophecies concerning the Messiah is that He would suffer. We can see hints of it very early in the Old Testament; some see indications in Abel's sacrifice and in Abraham's offering of Isaac. Without question we can see the suffering Savior typified in the Passover. But for extraordinary detail and vividness, no passage stands out as much as Isaiah 53, sometimes referred to as the "prophecy of the Suffering Messiah." We will look at only three of its specific prophecies, but the entire chapter is so exact that to read it is as if you were reading history and not an account of something yet to take place.

Before turning to the first of its prophecies that we will include in our examination, I'd like to notice J. Sidlow Baxter's comments about Isaiah 53 from his work, *Explore the Book*:

> It has been truly said the "prolonged description of chapter 53 suits only one figure in all of human history – the Man of Calvary." The following twelve points absolutely confirm this, for in their totality they cannot possibly be applied to any other. (1) He comes in utter lowliness – "a root out of a dry ground," etc. (2) He is "despised and rejected of men," etc. (3) He suffered for the sins and in the place of others – "He was wounded for our transgressions," etc. (4) It was God Himself who caused the suffering to be vicarious – "The Lord hath laid on Him the iniquity of us all." (5) There was an absolute resignation under the vicarious suffering – "He was afflicted, yet He opened not His mouth," etc. (6) He died as a felon – "He was taken from prison and from judgment." (7) He was cut off prematurely – "He was cut off out of the land of the living," etc. (8) Yet he was personally guiltless – "He had done no violence, neither was any deceit in His mouth." (9) And he was to live on after His sufferings – "He shall see His seed; He shall prolong His days." (10) Jehovah's pleasure was then to prosper in His hand – "The pleasure of Jehovah shall prosper in His hand." (11) He was to enter into mighty triumph after His suffering – "He shall divide the spoil with the strong," etc. (12) By all this, and by "justifying man" through His death and living again, He was to "see the travail of His soul, and be satisfied" (253-254).

3. Dumb Before Accusers – Isaiah 53:7

He was oppressed and He was afflicted, yet He did not open His mouth; like a lamb that is led to slaughter, and like a sheep that is silent before its shearers, so He did not open His mouth (Isa. 53:7).

Having already addressed the Messianic nature of Isaiah 53, we turn our attention to verse 7. It brings to mind the voluntary nature of the suffering the Promised One was to endure. He was oppressed, probably referring to the exaction of the penalty for the sins of man. His suffering would be borne patiently. There would be no threats coming forth from the Promised One, no abuse and no reviling would be heard from the Suffering Messiah.

Fulfillment – Matthew 27:12-14

And while He was being accused by the chief priests and elders, He did not answer. Then Pilate said to Him, "Do You not hear how many things they testify against You?" And He did not answer him with regard to even a single charge, so the governor was quite amazed (Matt. 27:12-14).

Accusation after accusation was leveled at Jesus; yet as Isaiah had prophesied, He opened not His mouth. Jesus did speak during this mockery of a trial, but He did not reply to a single one of the false charges brought against Him. His patient endurance brings to mind 1 Peter's 2:22-23. These verses act as inspired interpretation of Isaiah 53:7. Peter wrote:

Who committed no sin, nor was any deceit found in His mouth; and while being reviled, He did not revile in return; while suffering, He uttered no threats, but kept entrusting Himself to Him who judges righteously (1 Pet. 2:22-23).

Apparently Pilate had never seen such a prisoner before. Matthew tells us that he was "quite amazed." Death faced our Lord, yet He remained calm and collected, meek and yet so undeniably dignified.

4. Wounded and Bruised – Isaiah 53:5

But He was pierced through for our transgressions, He was crushed for our iniquities; the chastening for our well-being fell upon Him, and by His scourging we are healed (Isa. 53:5).

We will present a few comments from Jamieson, Fausset, and Brown's *Commentary on the Whole Bible*: "Of 'wounded' we read: 'a bodily wound; not mere mental sorrow; lit., 'pierced'; minutely appropriate to Messiah, whose hands, feet, and side were pierced.' Of 'bruised' we read: 'crushing inward and outward suffering.' Of 'stripes' we find: 'minutely prophetical of His being scourged" (578).

Isaiah 53:3 details the vicarious suffering of the Messiah. He would bear upon Himself the transgressions of all people and endure the punishment due them. This punishment was not the result of His own sins, for He had none. It was for the sins of others.

Fulfillment – Matthew 27:26

Then he released Barabbas for them; but after having Jesus scourged, he handed Him over to be crucified (Matt. 27:26).

Pilate gave orders for Jesus to be scourged. I believe from this and other passages that Pilate intend for the scourging to be the complete punishment. Often a prisoner would die while the scourging was taking place. The scourge was a many-thonged whip with pieces of bone or metal attached to the end of each thong. This instrument would be brought down time after time upon the stretched back, buttocks, and legs of the one being beaten. The prisoner would have been stripped of his clothing and fastened to a low post, thus bending the back and stretching the skin, exposing it to the cruelty of the whip. The Jews had a custom of forty stripes, save one. This was for fear of killing the one being beaten. Those executing the beating of Jesus, however, were not Jews. They were Romans, and no one knows how many stripes Jesus received.

The Pulpit Commentary presents these thoughts for our reflection: "To think that the blessed Son of God was subject to such torture and indignity is indeed a lesson for us written in blood. When 'he gave his back to the smiters' (Isaiah 50:6), he was taking the punishment of our sin upon his sacred shoulders" (XV: 586).

5. Rejected By His Own People – Isaiah 53:3

He was despised and forsaken of men, a man of sorrows and acquainted with grief; and like one from whom men hide their face He was despised, and we did not esteem Him (Isa. 53:3).

The Messiah would be one forsaken of men, characterized by sorrow and acquainted with calamity. He would be rejected by mankind in general, as one before whom men hid their faces; and more specifically, He would be rejected by the Jews. By use of the pronoun "we," Isaiah identifies himself with the Jews.

Fulfillment – John 19:14-15

Now it was the day of preparation for the Passover; it was about the sixth hour. And he said to the Jews, "Behold, your King!" So they cried out, "Away with Him, away with Him, crucify Him!" Pilate said to them, "Shall I crucify your King?" The chief priests answered, "We have no king but Caesar" (John 19:14-15).

There are many New Testament passages to which we could have referred that clearly demonstrate that Jesus was rejected by His own people – passages such as John 7:5 where we find, "For not even His brothers were believing in Him." We could also look at verses 47-49 of the same chapter, "The Pharisees then answered them, 'You have not also been led astray, have you? No one of the rulers or Pharisees has believed in Him, has he?'" Think also of the "rejected cornerstone" passages such as Matthew 21:42-43, all of which show the fulfillment of Isaiah 53:3.

Jesus came unto His own people, but they did not believe on Him. John 1:11 tells us, "He came to His own, and those who were His own did not receive Him." Now whether that is referring to the Jews specifically, or mankind in general, the point is made.

6. Smitten and Spat Upon – Isaiah 50:6

I gave My back to those who strike Me, and My cheeks to those who pluck out the beard; I did not cover My face from humiliation and spitting (Isa 50:6).

The messianic view of this passage has been almost universally accepted. It certainly was the view of the early church. In Isaiah 50, beginning with verse 4, the Messiah is pictured as doing the speaking. He makes it known that He comes forth from Jehovah, that He was sent with a task to perform and the power to do it. This He willingly undertook and would patiently endure the suffering and shame that came upon Him. This suffering and shame is the subject of Isaiah 50:6.

Concerning this particular passage, Hengstenberg states in *Christology of the Old Testament*:

> Although this was in part especially fulfilled in Christ, yet these particular traits, according to the custom of the Hebrew poets to particularize everything, served in the first instance for the contemporaries of the Prophet to express the thought, that the Messiah would experience, and patiently endure, the most shameful and abusive treatment. But God so directed the event, that even these special traits occurred again in the history of the Messiah. . . .To pluck out the beard is the greatest of all indignities in the East. . . .To spit, even in the presence of any one, in the East, is considered as an insult. But how much more to spit in one's face? (227)

Fulfillment – Matthew 26:67-68

Then they spat in His face and beat Him with their fists; and others slapped Him, and said, "Prophesy to us, You Christ; who is the one who hit you?" (Matt. 26:67-68).

The prophet had foretold that the Messiah would endure the greatest of indignities, and so He did. Jesus resigned Himself to being buffeted, to being spit upon (even today, a sign of utter disgust and contempt), in order that all men might be saved.

We need not wonder if there is some other meaning that can be correctly applied to Isaiah 50:6. Our Lord removed all doubt in Luke 18:31-32. That passage says, "Then he took the twelve aside and said to them, 'Behold, we are going up to Jerusalem, and all the things which are written through the prophets about the Son of Man will be accomplished. For He will be handed over to the Gentiles, and will be mocked, and mistreated, and spit upon.'"

We simply must go into further detail, and I have chosen to do so now, about the mockery of a trial that Jesus was forced to go through after His arrest in the garden of Gethsemane. He was first taken to the house of Annas. Annas was an older man who had been high priest, but had been removed from that office by the Romans. The

Romans had placed Caiaphas, the son-in-law of Annas, in his former position. The Jews regarded Annas as the legitimate high priest, because, according to Number 20:28 and 35:25, the office of high priest was held for life. Annas exercised considerable influence, not only with the Jews in general, but with his son-in-law, the "official" high priest.

I believe that Jesus was taken to Annas first for a two-fold purpose: (1) To gain the sanction of the legitimate high priest in the eyes of the people for the action they had planned; (2) To question Jesus for the purpose of gaining some information that could be used against Him in framing a suitable accusation before the Romans. It always seems to be the case that lacking truth and credible testimony, wicked men turn to violence to sustain their cause. One of the officers of the temple struck Jesus. The Greek word for "struck" shows that what Jesus received was "a slap on the cheek, given with the open hand by way of insulting rebuke rather than with the intention of inflicting bodily injury."

Jesus was led from Annas to the trial before Caiaphas. It would have been in a hall that was sufficiently large to accommodate the Sanhedrin, which had now come together. This was not a formal session as a court; it was more like a committee or a caucus. Caiaphas sought to force Jesus to give some evidence against Himself. With cunning and effrontery Caiaphas assumed that the testimony already given was all that could possibly be desired, and demanded of Jesus what He had to say in response to it. But Jesus gave him no answer. He gave him no explanation.

In desperation Caiaphas asked Jesus plainly and bluntly. His question was two-fold: (1) Are You the Christ? (2) Are You the Son of God? The latter would constitute blasphemy, the former, by showing a boastful spirit, would tend to confirm the charge. It could also be that Caiaphas anticipated the future and foresaw how useful this claim to be the Messiah would prove when the hearing before Pilate took place.

We should note that Caiaphas had no legal right to ask either of those questions. No man can be compelled to testify against Himself, but he knew the claims of Jesus, and realized that, if Jesus repudiated them He would be shamed forever, and if He asserted them He could be charged with blasphemy. Taking advantage of the situation, Caiaphas put the question to Jesus with the usual formula of an oath. This gave more power to the question because under ordinary circumstances a person was held to be guilty if he refused to answer a question put to him in that manner.

Jesus freely confessed the truth. "Right hand of power" was commonly understood to mean the right hand of God. By the words "nevertheless" and "hereafter" Jesus brought His present state of humiliation into contrast with His future state of glory. Hard as it might be for his accusers to believe it, the day would come when He would sit in judgment and they would stand on trial before Him.

Even though Jesus' answer was exactly what Caiaphas wanted to hear, he still pretended to be shocked and dramatically tore his clothes. "Tearing his clothes, the high priest said, 'What further need do we have of witnesses? You have heard the blasphemy; how does it seem to you?' And they all condemned Him to be deserving of death" (Mark 14:63-64). This was not the final, formal sentence. It was the mere determination of the council. When Jesus was turned over to the soldiers after this examination, He was subjected to ridicule and humiliation. He was spat upon, struck, and taunted, all taking place on Thursday evening.

And then on Friday morning, the Sanhedrin came together to formally charge Jesus and condemn Him. By law the Sanhedrin could meet as a council only in the daytime. All the preliminary work had been done. In truth, they had already condemned the Lord. Their coming together at this time was only to make their decisions final and give it the appearance of legitimacy. The determined steps were taken, the predetermined verdict reached, and then, having tried and condemned the Lord but having no legal power to put Him to death, the Sanhedrin needed a concurring sentence from the Roman governor. They would be taking Jesus to Pilate.

The trial before Pilate was held in the "praetorium," the official residence of the Roman governor. Traditionally it is believed that Pilate had his headquarters in the Tower of Antonia that overlooked the temple area from the northwest. Archeologists have uncovered a beautiful mosaic pavement under the present building that many think may have been the original Roman Court Room.

It appears that the original intention of the Jewish leaders was to get Pilate to accept their verdict and condemn Jesus solely on that basis. It is interesting that Pilate placated the Jewish leaders by going outside to hear the charges and then questioning Jesus inside the praetorium. The leaders would not go inside for fear of defiling themselves, yet the most defiling thing that they were doing had nothing to do with their location. It was the cruel and unjust sentence they were seeking, the death of the Son of God. When Pilate heard the initial charges, he told the Jewish leaders to pronounce their own sentence, but that would not have served their purpose. It was illegal for them to pronounce a death sentence, and a death sentence was what their verdict called for. Jesus could be legally put to death only by the Romans, and crucifixion was the mode by which such a sentence was carried out. Thus unwittingly, the Sanhedrin, through its insistence on the death penalty, was bringing about the fulfillment of prophecy (Isa. 53, Psa. 22).

With this reaction of Pilate, the Jewish leaders changed their tactics. Now it became, "We found this man misleading our nation and forbidding to pay taxes to Caesar, and saying that He Himself is Christ, a King." An examination of the charge reveals what they were attempting to do. The first charge was extremely vague, purposely so. The second charge was deliberately false. Remember, "Give to Caesar the things that are Caesar's, and to God the things that are God's." The third charge, that Jesus claimed to be a king, was true; but not in the way they were using it. Their intent by these charges was to give the impression that Jesus was claiming to be a political king and thus have Him stand in rebellion to Caesar.

Pilate went into his residence to question Jesus privately. All four gospels record his first question, "Are You the King of the Jews?" Jesus responded by saying, "It is as you say." John tells us that Jesus asked Pilate, "Are you saying this on your own initiative, or did others tell you about Me?" It was apparent that Jesus had done something to incur the wrath of the leaders of His nation, but He showed Pilate that He was not seeking to usurp the throne of Caesar. His kingdom was not of an earthly nature, and indeed, it never would be. The Lord's statement in John 18:36, "But as it is, My kingdom is not of this realm," has been misconstrued by some to mean that at a later time His kingdom would be earthly. The phrase, "as it is" is logical, not temporal. It can be properly rendered, "Seeing it is so." Vine's *Expository Dictionary of New Testament Words* says of it, "Of logical sequence, often partaking also of the character of, now therefore, now however, as it is."

Yes, Jesus was a king, as He affirmed to Pilate, but it was the nature of His kingdom that Pilate needed to understand. Jesus had come into this world to bear witness to and to reveal truth. The Jewish leaders had refused to "hear His voice," in the sense of accepting His words and obeying them. They had refused to recognize the spiritual nature of His kingdom. That was the problem.

Pilate's question, "What is truth?" has been viewed as a true, earnest question, as a despairing appeal, and as a sneer. I don't really know which it is. But I do know that, instead of waiting for Jesus to answer, Pilate went back out to the Jews to inform them that, as a result of his questioning, he had found no fault in Jesus.

When additional charges were leveled against Jesus by the Jews, Pilate sought to get the Lord to defend Himself. Yet Jesus would not respond to these false charges. His refusal to speak in His own defense caused Pilate to marvel, but the charges kept coming.

When Pilate heard that Jesus had begun in Galilee, he saw it as an opportunity to shift the case to another court. Herod was in Jerusalem for the Passover celebration. Luke says he was "in Jerusalem at that time," "that time" referring to the Passover season. While Herod was not a religious person, showing respect for the

Jewish festivals was important to his position. Pilate readily used this opportunity.

At an earlier period of the Lord's ministry, Herod was so troubled by a guilty conscience due to his murder of John the Baptist that reports of the work of Jesus had frightened him. Herod thought that Jesus might have been John risen from the dead. This indicates that the fear had passed, and now he was curious about Jesus. He had heard that Jesus performed miracles and now he was thinking that he might get to see one. We have been given no indication of what Herod asked Jesus, but we know that the Lord remained quiet before him.

The chief priests and the scribes vehemently accused Jesus before Herod, but the Lord answered nothing. Evidently the silence of Jesus angered Herod, for he and his soldiers subsequently treated Jesus with abusive contempt by mocking Him and dressing Him in a royal robe. Finally Herod sent Jesus back to Pilate, having found nothing worthy of condemnation.

When Jesus was sent back to Pilate, Pilate called together the chief priests and the rulers of the people. He told them once again that he had found no fault in Jesus. Even Herod had found nothing worthy of death. So Pilate gave them the chance to have Jesus beaten severely and then released, as per the custom of releasing a prisoner at the time of the feast. The Roman government did its best to suppress the turbulent elements in the provinces under their control. The release of a political prisoner at the great feast of the Jews was one concession to the conquered nation that they hoped would calm the seeds of rebellion. The people were already gathering to demand the release; here was a good opportunity. They would get Jesus punished and Pilate would not find it necessary to have Him killed.

The choice was limited to Barabbas or Jesus. It seems as though Pilate chose Barabbas because he was such a notorious person who could not possibly stir the sympathy of the people, and they would demand the release of Jesus. The leaders of the Jews intervened and persuaded the people to demand the release of Barabbas and the crucifixion of the innocent Jesus. When Pilate presented the people with the choice, they cried out, "Barabbas." When asked about Jesus, they said, "Crucify, crucify Him!" Pilate said to the crowd, "Why, what evil has this man done? I have found in Him no guilt demanding death; therefore I will punish Him and release Him." Pilate then gave orders for Jesus to be scourged.

After the beating, the Lord was crowned with a crown of thorns by the soldiers. A purple garment, the color of royalty, was thrown about Him. He was tormented by the soldiers and struck by their hands.

Once more Pilate went before the people, prepared to bring Jesus out before them, telling them once again that he had found no crime in Him. Jesus came forth, beaten, crowned with thorns, and wearing the purple garment. Pilate cried out, "Behold the man!" Surely this would stimulate some sympathy from the people as they viewed the pathetic sight before them. Yet the chief priests and the officers, upon seeing Jesus, cried out, "Crucify Him, crucify Him!"

Pilate responded, "Take Him yourselves and crucify Him, for I find no fault in Him!" In response the Jewish leaders now gave the real charge, "He made Himself out to be the Son of God."

Again Pilate returned to his residence to question Jesus further. John tells us that he was "more afraid." He asked Jesus, "Who are you? Where are you from?" Jesus gave him no answer. Again Pilate spoke, "You do not speak to me? Do you not know that I have authority to release you, and I have authority to crucify you?" Our Lord's reply to this shows that the matter wasn't really in Pilate's hands at all, except by the deliberate choice of God. Pilate had no real acquaintance with Jesus other than what was happening right then. But the leaders of the Jews had many opportunities to know better. They had personal knowledge of Jesus. They knew what He had done and what He had taught. They knew the prophecies of the prophets. Yet they were rejecting Jesus outright and delivering Him for death. Of whom much is given, much is expected.

After this exchange Pilate sought even more to release Jesus, only to be threatened with an appeal to Caesar on the issue of his having set a man free who had been arrested on the charge of claiming to be a king and appearing as a rival of Caesar. With this new threat Pilate determined that it was now time for this trial to come to an end. Back and forth it had gone – in the residence, then back outside with the Jews. Now the final verdict was to be rendered. It took place in the place called "the Pavement" – evidently a spot for such an act located in the front of the palace. He told the Jews, "Behold your king!" They cried out, "Away with Him, away with Him. Crucify Him!" Pilate said, "Shall I crucify your king?" And the chief priests answered, "We have no king but Caesar!"

Pilate then called for a basin of water and symbolically washed his hands of the blood of Jesus saying, "I am innocent of this man's blood." To which the Jewish people replied, "His blood be on us, and on our children."

It was about 6:00 a.m. Friday morning (John 19:14, using the Roman method of keeping time). Finally, from fear and lack of courage, Pilate released Barabbas and delivered Jesus to be crucified.

7. Hated Without Cause – Psalm 69:4

Those who hate me without a cause are more than the hairs of my head; those who would destroy me are powerful, what I did not steal, I then have to restore (Psa. 69:4).

The 69th Psalm is a psalm of David and contains much that pertains only to him. We need not go very far into the psalm, however, to find someone else referred to as well – that being the suffering Savior. David faced many trials in his life; so did Jesus. David had many enemies; so did Jesus. David often cried against his enemies, and this psalm is filled with such imprecations; Jesus prayed for His. But in the situation described in verse 4, we see a type of the Lord.

In *The Treasury of David*, Spurgeon wrote:

Surprising in that men should hate the altogether lovely one, truly is it added, "without a cause," for reason there was none for this senseless enmity. He neither blasphemed God, nor injured man. As Samuel said: "Whose ox have I taken? Or whose ass have I taken? Or whom have I defrauded? Whom have I oppressed?" Even so might Jesus inquire. Besides, he had not only done us no evil, but he had bestowed countless and priceless benefits. . . .Yet from his cradle to his cross, beginning with Herod and now ending with Judas, he had foes without number; and he justly said, they "are more than hairs of mine head!" (III: 260).

Fulfillment – John 15:24-25

If I had not done among them the works which no one else did, they would not have sin; but now they have both seen and hated Me and My Father as well. But they have done this in order that the word may be fulfilled that is written in their Law, "They hated Me without a cause" (John 15:24-25).

Here Jesus quotes Psalm 69:4 and applies it to Himself and the unfounded animosity felt toward Him by so many. He came but to save the world, but the world, for the most part, hated Him.

Chapter 15 of the gospel of John closes with a contrast of the love of believers one to another and the hatred of the world. The world, once again for the most part, hated the Lord, some out of ignorance, others out of willful malice and neglect. Both were without excuse. They had seen the Lord, heard the Lord, and witnessed His works. They were guilty of rejecting the Messiah. But since the world hated the Lord, His followers should not have been surprised when they were hated as well. Jesus said in verse 20, "Remember the word that I said to you, 'A slave is not greater than his master.' If they persecuted Me, they will also persecute you; if they kept My word, they will keep yours also."

Chapter Eight
Prophecies Concerning His Death

In 1 Corinthians 15:3 the Apostle Paul wrote, "For I delivered unto you first of all that which I also received, how that Christ died for our sins according to the scriptures." In his famous sermon in Acts 2, Peter stated in verse 23, "This Man, delivered over by the predetermined plan and foreknowledge of God, you nailed to a cross by the hands of godless men and put Him to death."

The death of the Messiah is the subject of this chapter. It was not an accident; it was not a mistake. Jesus was delivered by the predetermined counsel and foreknowledge of God. He died on the cross so that all men might have the opportunity to be saved, all "according to the scriptures."

1. Crucified With Thieves – Isaiah 53:12

Therefore will I divide him a portion with the great and he shall divide the spoil with the strong; because he hath poured out his soul unto death: and he was numbered with the transgressors; and he bore the sin of many, and made intercession for the transgressors (Isa. 53:12).

The Promised Messiah was not a transgressor, but He often would be treated as one. He would be numbered, or accounted, with malefactors and law-breakers. Indeed, in the life of Jesus He was numbered with transgressors many times. Jesus was accused of being a Sabbath-breaker, a blasphemer, and a friend of publicans and sinners. But never was this statement of Isaiah more clearly fulfilled than in the event that took place on Calvary.

Fulfillment – Mark 15:27-28

They crucified two robbers with Him, one on His right and one on His left. And the Scripture was fulfilled which says, "And He was numbered with transgressors" (Mark 15:27-28).

When taken together, all of the gospel accounts of the crucifixion of Jesus make it apparent that, at the beginning, both of the robbers crucified with the Lord taunted Him; but one of them repented, and thus we have the memorable account of the thief on the cross. The dignified conduct of Jesus on the cross must have made a tremendous impression on the penitent thief. As a matter of fact, his was the only voice to be raised in protest to the death of Jesus. His statement of Luke 23:42, "Jesus, remember me when You come in Your kingdom," certainly indicates belief in Jesus and a belief, however primitive it might have been, that Jesus would continue on. He didn't ask to be removed from the cross, but to be "remembered" when Jesus came into His kingdom. Someone once wrote, "Some saw Jesus raise the dead, and did not believe; the robber sees Jesus put to death, and yet believes."

The Lord's response was, "Truly I say to you, today you shall be with Me in Paradise." It is such a shame that the thief has become the favorite of those who attempt to circumvent the command to be baptized for the remission of sins. Baptism for the remission of sins is into the death of Jesus (Rom. 6:3-5). While on earth, Jesus could forgive sins as He saw fit (Matt. 9:5-6). Having not yet died, Jesus personally forgave this man his sins. After His death and resurrection, and His ascension to heaven, all sins must be forgiven according to the terms of His will, the New Testament. Both the thief and Jesus lived and died under the Old Law.

2. Friends Stand Afar Off – Psalm 38:11

My loved ones and my friends stand aloof from my plague; and my kinsmen stand afar off (Psa. 38:11).

Psalm 38 is called a "Psalm of David, to bring to remembrance." Just exactly at what point in David's life it was written, we cannot say. It is obvious that in it David expresses the feeling of being forgotten and forsaken by his closest associates. He recounts his sorrows and cries for help to endure them. Surely, in verse 11, we find in David's standing alone a type of what happened to Jesus.

A.R. Fausett, in *A Commentary Critical, Experimental and Practical on the Old and New Testaments,* wrote of verse 11:

> At the very time when my affliction would have required them to stand nearer and more steadily by me than ever, they are afraid of the danger that they would incur by seeming to take part with me. While the enemies are near, the friends are far. So in the case of Messiah (III: 184).

Fulfillment – Luke 23:49
And all his acquaintances and the women who accompanied Him from Galilee, were standing at a distance, seeing these things (Luke 23:49).

The women and others of Jesus' acquaintance stood afar off and gazed upon Him as He hung on the cross.

Psalm 22
We are now going to be turning our attention to prophecies found in the twenty-second psalm. We will be looking at six in our study. Just as the 53rd chapter of the book of Isaiah presents the picture of the Suffering Messiah in startling and graphic detail, the twenty-second psalm presents the picture of the cross. Our hearts are wrenched by the agony found in its words, yet our spirits are lifted by the expressions of praise and glory found in it as well.

C.H. Spurgeon gives a marvelous synopsis of the Psalm in *The Treasury of David.* He wrote:

> This is beyond all others The Psalm of The Cross. It may have been actually repeated word by word by our Lord when hanging on the tree; it would be too bold to say that it was so, but even a casual reader may see that it might have been. It begins with, "My God, my God, why hast thou forsaken me?" and ends, according to some, in the original with "It is finished." For plaintive expressions uprising from unutterable depths of woe we may say of this psalm, "There is none like it." It is the photograph of our Lord's saddest hours, the record of

his dying words, the lachrymatory of his last tears, the memorial of his expiring joy. David and his afflictions may be here in a very modified sense, but, as the star is concealed by the light of the sun, he who sees Jesus will probably neither see nor care to see David. Before us we have a description of the darkness and of the glory of the cross, the sufferings of Christ and the glory which shall follow (I, #365).

3. Forsaken – Psalm 22:1

My God, my God, why have You forsaken me? Far from my deliverance are the words of my groaning (Psa. 22:1).

Can we see David in this statement? Perhaps. There may have been many times in his life while fleeing from Saul or contending with his rebellious son, Absalom, while hiding in a cave or elsewhere fearing for his very life, that David was moved to feel forsaken by God. He may have felt that way, but he was not. This prophecy has a much higher significance, an ultimate fulfillment. Its subject is the Messiah.

In David's words, we feel the anguish of being alone. In Christ, that anguish is realized.

Fulfillment – Matthew 27:46

And about the ninth hour Jesus cried out with a loud voice, saying, "Eli, Eli, lama sabachtani?" that is, "My God, My God, why have You forsaken Me?" (Matt. 27:46).

Yes, David wrote these words, but they reached their ultimate fulfillment many years later as the Son of David hung on the cross. There need be no question as to their fulfillment. The words of Jesus demand it. In their context, both Matthew and Mark tell us that it was about 3:00 in the afternoon when Jesus cried out, "My God, My God, why have You forsaken Me?" As we have seen, this is a quote from Psalm 22:1, but it is a great deal more than that. We know that God turns from sin (Isa. 59:1-2). We know that there is no fellowship between God and the unfruitful works of darkness (2 Cor. 6:14-16). We know as well, based upon 2 Corinthians 5:21, that Jesus was made to be sin for us. I believe that Jesus was bearing the weight of all of the sins of the world combined in one incomprehensibly horrific mass and that the Father was turning from it. Jesus bore that terrible weight alone. His anguish was real and beyond our limited understanding or appreciation. He was there in my stead. It is important that we understand that God the Father was not turning His back on His Son, our Lord and Savior Jesus Christ. In fact, there was never a time in Jesus' life when God was more pleased with Him.

4. The Broken Heart – Psalm 22:14

I am poured out like water, and all my bones are out of joint; my heart is like wax; it is melted within me (Psa. 22:14).

The essence of this prophecy regards the physical condition of the Messiah on the cross. He was totally spent. His life-sustaining blood had poured forth since the crowning with thorns and the merciless scourging. He had poured forth as water and His strength was gone; there was but little left to sustain Him.

Jamieson, Fausett, and Brown describe this verse in this fashion in their *Commentary on the Whole Bible:* "Utter exhaustion and hopeless weakness, in these circumstances of pressing danger, are set forth by the most expressive figures; the solidity of the body is destroyed, and it becomes like water; the bones are parted; the heart, the very seat of vitality, melts like wax" (415).

Fulfillment – John 19:34

But one of the soldiers pierced His side with a spear, and immediately blood and water came out (John 19:34).

Some hold that this was a result of a build-up of a colorless fluid in the pericardium brought on by the continued and intense suffering endured by our Lord; others find in it evidence of a ruptured heart. However one views it, it is obvious that the words, "My heart is like wax; it is melted within me" find their fulfillment in the crucifixion of our Lord.

5. Hands and Feet Pierced – Psalm 22:16

For dogs have surrounded me; a band of evildoers has encompassed me; they pierced my hands and my feet (Psa. 22:16).

How remarkable is this prophecy, especially when we pause to remember that the manner in which the death sentence was carried out at the time of its writing was by stoning. Even if we consider death at the hands of one's enemies in battle, piercing of the hands and feet would be most unusual.

No, the Holy Spirit, through David, was looking many years into the future and seeing the Son of God hanging on the cross, crucified after the manner of the Romans, pierced in both hands and feet.

Hengstenberg, in *Christology of the Old Testament*, writes, "These words, however, can refer neither to David, nor to any other sufferer except the Messiah; since, as Gesenius remarks, 'Men pierced indeed the body of their enemy, but not his hands and feet.' They rather refer to Christ, who, as a consequence of the punishment of the cross, endured this suffering" (82).

Fulfillment – Luke 23:33

When they came to the place called The Skull, there they crucified Him and the criminals, one on the right and the other on the left (Luke 23:33).

The crucifixion site was outside the city walls but near to the city. Hebrews 13:12 and John 19:20 are specific about that, and Matthew 27:32, as well as John 19:17, certainly imply it. The exact location of this site is not known, although it has been the topic of much conjecture and tradition. Why it was "The place called The Skull" has also been a matter of considerable debate. Two plausible explanations have been offered: (1) Skulls had been found at this particular location; (2) More likely it was so called because it was a hill that had a physical makeup giving it the appearance of a skull. No one knows for sure.

Jesus was crucified by Roman soldiers according to the customary Roman method. This involved being nailed to the cross, both hands and feet. The statement of our Lord to Thomas in John 20:27 further illustrates that He had been "nailed" to the cross.

The *International Standard Bible Encyclopedia* provides us with this description of the agony of crucifixion:

The suffering of death by crucifixion was intense, especially in hot climates. Severe local inflammation, coupled with an insignificant bleeding of the jagged wounds, produced traumatic fever, which was aggravated by the exposure to the heat of the sun, the strained position of the body and the insufferable thirst. The wounds swelled about the rough nails and the torn and lacerated tendons and nerves caused excruciating agony. The arteries of the head and stomach were surcharged with blood and a terrific throbbing headache ensued. The mind was confused and filled with anxiety and dread foreboding. The victim of crucifixion literally died a thousand deaths. Tetanus not rarely supervened and the rigors of the attending convulsions would tear at the wounds and add to the burden of pain, till at last the bodily forces were exhausted and the victim sank to unconsciousness and death (II: 761).

This is what the sinless Savior of man endured.

6. Mocked – Psalm 22:7-8

All who see me sneer at me; they separate with the lip, they wag the head, saying, "Commit yourself to the Lord; let Him deliver him; let Him rescue him, because He delights in him" (Psa. 22:7-8).

The subject of this prophecy would be subjected to the cruelest of ridicule; gestures of contempt would rain upon him. Even the sustaining faith that He had in God would be used by His tormentors in the most diabolical taunt of all. We do not question that David was the object of ridicule by his enemies. Perhaps even his faith was used against him. But David is not the ultimate subject of Psalm 22:7-8. These words find their fulfillment in the Messiah.

Fulfillment – Matthew 27:39-43

And those passing by were hurling abuse at Him, wagging their heads and saying, "You who are going to destroy the temple and rebuild it in three days, save Yourself! If you are the Son of God, come down from the cross." In the same way the chief priests also, along with the scribes and elders, were mocking Him and saying, "He saved others; He cannot save Himself. He is the King of Israel; let Him now come down from the cross, and we will believe in Him. He trusts in God; let God rescue Him now, if He delights in Him; for He said, 'I am the Son of God'" (Matt. 27:39-43).

With amazing accuracy the words of Psalm 22:7-8 come to pass. The Son of God hangs on the cross as an object of scorn, contempt, and ridicule.

Again, from *Christology of the Old Testament* we find:

> Both passages so literally correspond, that the resemblance cannot possibly be regarded as the result of accident. Michaelis has very properly remarked: "They quoted from this Psalm (as people are accustomed to do, who are much conversant with the Bible), because its language harmonized with their sentiments, without being aware of its character, and how unhappily for themselves they were fulfilling its predictions." But even were we to suppose that the revilers of Christ used these words independently of the Psalm, still the coincidence in which this agreement consists, Matthew designed to lead his reader to the conviction, that in the sufferings of Christ, the most remarkable predictions of the Old Testament respecting the Messiah's sufferings, were completely fulfilled" (81).

7. Stared At – Psalm 22:17

I can count all my bones. They look, they stare at me (Psa. 22:17).

As a result of the suffering endured, the skin of the subject of the psalm would be pulled tight, allowing even for the numbering of the bones. The eyes of many would fall upon Him, but they would not be eyes filled with sympathy and tenderness. This does not refer to David; it refers to Christ.

Fulfillment – Luke 23:35a

And the people stood by, looking on (Luke 23:35a).

The word from which "looking on" is translated is the same word from which we get the word "spectator." Vine's *Expository Dictionary of New Testament Words* defines it as, "used of one who looks at a thing with interest and for a purpose, usually indicating the careful observation of details."

At scenes of tragedy and death, people will stand and stare. They did then, and people are no different now. Jesus hung on the cross as an object for spectators, something for them to stare at. Considering His physical condition and the fact that He was probably clothed only in a loincloth (out of deference for Jewish custom), to be gazed at intently would have been occasion for great embarrassment. The man who brought the highest moral standard ever known to man was made an object for the imprudently curious to stare at.

8. Garments Parted and Lots Cast – Psalm 22:18

They divide my garments among them, and for my clothing they cast lots (Psa. 22:18).

When an individual was crucified, his garments became the property of the ones doing the crucifixion, at least in most cases. Parting garments among those responsible was not unusual, but casting lots over them was. The fact that this action was out of the ordinary, and yet precisely what happened in the case of Jesus, demonstrates that David was not speaking of himself but of the one who would be called the Son of David.

Fulfillment – John 19:23-24

Then the soldiers, when they had crucified Jesus, took His outer garments and made four parts, a part to every soldier and also the tunic; now the tunic was seamless, woven in one piece. So they said to one another, "Let us not tear it, but cast lots for it, to decide whose it shall be." This was to fulfill the Scripture: "They divided My outer garments among them, and for My clothing they cast lots" (John 19:23-24).

Since God's word is the only infallible interpreter of prophecy, we do not have to wonder about what or whom Psalm 22:18 refers. It finds its fulfillment in the parting of the garments and the casting of the lots. Roman law awarded the clothes of the crucified individual to the soldiers of the crucifixion party, in this case a quaternion of Roman soldiers (four soldiers – John 19:23). Having finished the crucifixion, the soldiers divided the part of the Lord's garments that could be divided into four parts, a part for each of the soldiers. For his coat or robe, the outer garment, they cast lots; for it was without seam and to divide it would have ruined it. An interesting aspect of this event is brought out by Homer Hailey in *That You May Believe – Studies in the Gospel of John*, where he wrote:

The *contrast* between the tenderness of Him who had loved so fully and warmly and who even now of His own will was laying down His life for others, and the hardness of those who were crucifying Him is demonstrated in their manner of disposing of His garments. Of His regular garments it is said that they divided them; but of the special outer garment, made without seam, they said, "Let us not rend it, but cast lots for it, whose it shall be": that the scripture might be fulfilled, which saith, "They parted my raiment among them, and for my vesture they did cast lots. These things therefore the soldiers did." They were so unimpressed by the scene that they could indifferently spend their time in this way.

9. Suffers Thirst – Psalm 69:21
10. Gall and Vinegar Offered – Psalm 69:21

They also gave me gall for my food and for my thirst they gave me vinegar to drink (Psa. 69:21).

As we noticed in the preceding chapter, Psalm 69 is a Psalm of David in which David bemoans his afflictions and calls for the destruction of his enemies. But David is not alone in this psalm, for in it we find the Messiah, the Crucified One. Much that is found in the psalm applies only to David. However, much of it applies to David only in an immediate, or temporary, sense, reaching its ultimate meaning in Christ.

Gall and vinegar are both most unpleasant to the taste, and their combination in this is remarkable considering what took place with our Lord during His crucifixion. Where perhaps sympathy should have been aroused, there was none. When refreshment was needed, only bitterness was given.

Fulfillment – Matthew 27:34; John 19:28-30

They gave Him wine to drink mixed with gall; and after tasting it, He was unwilling to drink (Matt. 27:34).

After this, Jesus, knowing that all things had already been accomplished, to fulfill the Scripture, said, "I am thirsty." A jar full of sour wine was standing there; so they put a sponge full of the sour wine upon a branch of hyssop and brought it up to His mouth. Therefore when Jesus had received the sour wine, He said, "It is finished!" And He bowed His head and gave up His spirit (John 19:28-30).

When they arrived at the crucifixion site, Jesus was offered a drink of wine mingled with gall and myrrh. It was intended to dull the senses of those being crucified and to lessen the agony. After tasting it, Jesus refused to drink. Having come to this point, the Lord would do nothing to ease the suffering or dull His pain.

I am reminded of the words of Psalm 22:15, "My strength is dried up like a potsherd, and my tongue cleaves to my jaws; and You lay me in the dust of death." With death but moments away, Jesus cried, "I am thirsty." Someone placed a sponge that had been soaked in the sour wine that the soldiers usually drank upon a reed and held it to the lips of Jesus. After having received the drink, Jesus cried with a loud voice, "It is finished!"

11. Committed Himself to God – Psalm 31:5

Into Your hand I commit my spirit; You have ransomed me, O Lord, God of truth (Psa. 31:5).

The 31st Psalm is a Psalm of David to the chief musician. It is a psalm that speaks of grief and trials and yet expresses trust and confidence in God, as well as thankfulness for mercies already received. Some feel that the psalm may have been occasioned by the treachery of the men of Keilah; others believe it to have been prompted by the rebellion of Absalom.

In verse 5 of this psalm we find another besides David; we find there the dying words of Jesus.

Fulfillment – Luke 23:46

And Jesus, crying out with a loud voice, said, "Father, into Your hands I commit My spirit." Having said this, He breathed His last (Luke 23:46).

In Psalm 31:5 David uttered those words that he might not die. Jesus spoke the same words as He died. He had come to do the will of His Father and His death on the cross was in keeping with that will. A greater, much deeper significance was attached to those words as Jesus uttered them in death. David cried to be preserved from death. Jesus cried forth as He acquiesced to it. Having said this, Jesus died, voluntarily yielding up His spirit.

12. Bones Not Broken – Psalm 34:20; Exodus 12:46
13. Side Pierced – Zechariah 12:10

He keeps all his bones, not one of them is broken (Psa. 34:20).

It is to be eaten in a single house; you are not to bring forth any of the flesh outside of the house, nor are you to break any bone of it (Exod. 12:46).

I will pour out on the house of David and on the inhabitants of Jerusalem, the Spirit of grace and of supplication, so that they will look on Me whom they have pierced; and they will mourn for Him, as one mourns for an only son, and they will weep bitterly over Him like the bitter weeping over a firstborn (Zech. 12:10).

This psalm commemorates a time in David's life when he feigned himself to be mad and so escaped from Achish the king of Gath. It is a psalm of praise to God for His deliverance, as well as a psalm of instruction concerning His care for His people.

In verse 20 we find an interesting statement as it regards David, as well as a prophecy that finds its exact fulfillment in Christ. Not one of David's bones was broken in the danger he faced. The same would be true of Jesus, even as He gave His life on the cross.

So as the Passover lamb was not to have a bone broken, as David suffered no broken bones, so too Jesus, contrary to custom surrounding crucifixion, suffered no broken bones.

Zechariah is one of the most highly messianic books in the Old Testament. It can be dated in the post-Exilic Period, roughly 520 B.C. and is contemporary with the book of Haggai. The pages of Zechariah contain much about the Promised One. He is found as "the Branch" of David, as a king, and as a shepherd. Zechariah looked beyond the immediate and the physical, which would be the rebuilding of the temple of God. He looked forward to the Messiah, to the spiritual house of God, and to the fulfillment of God's purpose. There would be considerable opposition, but God's purpose would triumph.

In Zechariah 12:10 we find the Messiah presented as the One

"whom they have pierced." Of this prophecy Homer Hailey, in *A Commentary on the Minor Prophets*, wrote:

> The strength through which Jehovah enables His saints to overcome and defeat their enemies is provided through His grace and their turning to Him in supplication. Therefore Jehovah promises to pour upon both the house of David and the inhabitants of Jerusalem the spirit of grace – divine unmerited favor – which would cause them to seek that which His grace provides. This spirit of grace would bring them to repentance and turn them to Him in supplication. They had rejected Jehovah in the person of the shepherd (ch. 11), and now they "pierce" Him in the person of His Son. "They shall look unto me whom they have pierced" is the authentic reading. They could not pierce Jehovah in the sense of putting Him to death; but they pierced Him through insult, blasphemy, and rejection. . . .What they had done to Jehovah, their descendants would do to His Son (390).

Fulfillment – John 19:32-37

So the soldiers came, and broke the legs of the first man and of the other who was crucified with Him; but coming to Jesus, when they saw that He was already dead, they did not break His legs. But one of the soldiers pierced His side with a spear, and immediately blood and water came out. And he who has seen has testified, and his testimony is true; and he knows that he is telling the truth, so that you also may believe. For these things came to pass to fulfill the Scripture, "Not a bone of Him shall be broken." And again another Scripture says, "They shall look on Him whom they pierced" (John 19:32-37).

This was the day before the Sabbath of the Passover Week, and because of the festivities and significance of the events taking place in this week, this Sabbath was a "high" or "great" day. The day before the Sabbath was called the "preparation." In the works of Josephus we find that the preparation for the Sabbath began on the ninth hour of the sixth day, 3:00 in the afternoon, according to the Jewish method of keeping time.

Not wanting the bodies to be hanging on the cross on the Sabbath, the Jewish leaders requested of Pilate that the legs of the crucified men be broken so that they would die quickly and could be taken down from the crosses. The way this was done was for the soldiers to use large clubs with which they would shatter the legs of the men, thus bringing their deaths almost immediately.

When the soldiers came to carry out their task, they broke the legs of the two criminals before they came to Jesus. Isn't it interesting that the soldiers took care of their gruesome task with the other two, even though Jesus was crucified between them? Coming to Jesus, the soldiers found that He was already dead. To ensure that they had not made a mistake, a soldier pierced the side of Jesus with a spear, and blood and water flowed out. Later John states clearly that he was there, that he saw it happen, and that his testimony of the matter is true. He wrote that he was writing of it so that those who read it could believe!

Even after His death, fulfillment of prophecies continued. John mentions, "A bone of him shall not be broken," from Exodus 12:46 and relating to the Passover Lamb. In the ultimate sense this referred to Jesus (1 Cor. 5:7). John also mentions, "They shall look on him whom they pierced" (Zech. 12:10).

14. Buried With Rich – Isaiah 53:9

His grave was assigned with wicked men, yet He was with a rich man in His death, because He had done no violence, nor was there any deceit in His mouth (Isa. 53:9).

The Suffering Messiah of Isaiah 53 was treated as a malefactor, and in death He would be assigned a grave with the wicked. The New American Standard Version reads, "His grave was assigned to be with wicked men." But it would not come to pass that the Messiah would be buried in the tombs of the common criminals and wicked men. He would be buried in the tomb of the rich.

Fulfillment – Mark 15:43-46

Joseph of Arimathea came, a prominent member of the Council, who himself was waiting for the kingdom of God; and he gathered up courage and went in before Pilate, and asked for the body of Jesus. Pilate wondered if He was dead by this time, and summoning the centurion, he questioned him as to whether He was already dead.

And ascertaining this from the centurion, he granted the body to Joseph. Joseph brought a linen cloth, took Him down, wrapped Him in the linen cloth and laid Him in a tomb which had been hewn out in the rock; and he rolled a stone against the entrance of the tomb (Mark 15:43-46).

By combining all of the gospel accounts concerning the Lord's burial, we find that a man by the name of Joseph of Arimathea stepped forward to request the body of Jesus. He was a member of the Sanhedrin who had not consented to their counsel and deeds concerning Jesus. He was a good and righteous man, and wealthy. He was all of these things, but John tells us that he was a "secret" disciple of Jesus for fear of his fellow Jewish leaders. He went to Pilate and requested the body of the Lord. When he did, Pilate was surprised that Jesus would be dead already. There are accounts of individuals living an entire week on the cross. Death on the first day was rare.

When Pilate received assurance that Jesus was truly dead from the centurion in charge, he released the body to Joseph. It is apparent that Joseph made his request for the body of Jesus alone, but he was assisted in the burial by Nicodemus, the same leader of the Jews who had first come to Jesus under the cover of night in John 3. He came with a mixture of myrrh and aloes, about 100 pounds, that they would use in the burial. Again, it is apparent that the two of them removed the body from the cross.

The linen cloth with which Jesus was wrapped for burial would actually have been torn into strips for winding around the body. John mentions "linen cloths," indicating the many strips used in the burial. The spices that Nicodemus brought would be placed between the folds of the linen in order to partially embalm the body. In the same area where the crucifixion had taken place there was a garden. In the garden there was a tomb that had never been used, a cave-like structure having been hewn out of rock, belonging to Joseph of Arimathea. In this tomb Jesus was laid, and a large stone was rolled to the door of the tomb. Joseph and Nicodemus left. The Sabbath Day was drawing near.

Thus far, we have seen, through prophecy, a picture of the birth, lineage, ministry, character, betrayal, suffering and death of the Promised One. It is a remarkably detailed picture. At this point, Jesus the Messiah was lying in the tomb of Joseph of Arimathea. But God be thanked that the story does not end this way.

Chapter Nine

Prophecies Concerning His Resurrection and Ascension

But now Christ has been raised from the dead, the first fruits of those who are asleep (1 Cor. 15:20).

Having left the Promised One in the tomb of the rich, the picture is incomplete. But the prophecies do not stop there. Yes, the promised Messiah would be betrayed. Yes, He would suffer. Yes, He would be crucified and buried. But He would rise and ascend to His father in heaven to live forevermore.

1. Resurrection – Psalm 16:10

For You will not abandon my soul to Sheol; nor will You allow Your Holy One to undergo decay (Psa. 16:10).

Psalm 16 is called the "Michtam of David," which is usually taken to mean, "The Golden Psalm of David." It is messianic in nature. That this is true is clearly pointed out by Peter's statement found in Acts 2:25 when he said, "For David says of Him" and then proceeds to quote from this psalm. Understanding that through the Holy Spirit David is speaking of the Messiah, we can readily grasp the significance of verse 10.

Spurgeon wrote in *The Treasury of David,* the following:

He declared his Father's faithfulness in the words "Thou wilt not leave my soul in hell," and that faithfulness was proven on the resurrection morning. Among the departed and disembodied Jesus was not left;

he had believed in the resurrection, and he received it on the third day, when his body rose in glorious life, according as he had said in joyous confidence, "Neither wilt thou suffer thine Holy One to see corruption" (I: 221).

Fulfillment – Acts 2:31

He looked ahead and spoke of the resurrection of the Christ, that He was neither abandoned to Hades, nor did His flesh suffer decay (Acts 2:31).

The actual resurrection of Jesus is not described in Scripture. We do not know exactly what took place when the Lord came forth from the grave. So we turn to Peter's reference to Psalm 16. David wrote of Sheol and Peter wrote of Hades. Literally, the word means, "the unseen," and refers to the abode of the dead. Peter's statement removed all doubt as to what Psalm 16:10 had reference to and when it was fulfilled.

In *New Commentary on Acts of Apostles,* J.W. McGarvey made some interesting observations concerning Peter's comments. He wrote:

> It was well known to the Jews, as it now is to all interpreters of the pro-phetic Psalms, that David habitually speaks in the first person when prophesying of the Christ; and in any given case, if it is made clear that he does not speak of himself, the conclusion is that he speaks of the Christ. This is the force of Peter's argument, and it proved to his Jewish hearers that which he set out to prove, that the Christ, accord-ing to a predetermined and expressed purpose of God, was to suffer death, and to arise again speedily from the dead (33).

2. Seated at the Right Hand of God – Psalm 110:1

The Lord says to my Lord: "Sit at My right hand until I make Your enemies a footstool for Your feet" (Psa. 110:1).

As we have already mentioned earlier in this work, the subject of Psalm 110 is the Priest/King. The kings of Israel, including David, did not combine these offices. It was to happen in one who was to come, in the One the Jews looked for as the Messiah.

Jamieson, Fausett, and Brown make the following remarks about Psalm 110:1 in their *Commentary on the Whole Bible.* Of "The Lord said," they write, "A formula used in prophetic or other solemn or express declarations." Of "My Lord," they say, "That the Jews understood this term to denote the Messiah their traditions show, and Christ's mode of arguing on such an assumption (Matthew 22:44) also proves." Concerning "Sit thou at my right hand," they say, "Not only a mark of honor, but also implied participation of power." And of "Until I make," they write, "The dominion of Christ over his enemies, as commissioned by God, and entrusted with all power (Matthew 28:18) for their subjugation, will assuredly be established (1 Corinthians 15:24-28)."

The Priest/King would ascend to the position of highest authority and power. He would ascend to sit at the right hand of God.

Fulfillment – Acts 2:33-35

Therefore having been exalted to the right hand of God, and having received from the Father the promise of the Holy Spirit, He has poured forth this which you both see and hear. For it was not David who ascended into heaven, but he himself says: "The Lord said to My Lord, sit at My right hand, until I make Your enemies a footstool for Your feet" (Acts 2:33-35).

Not only had the Messiah risen from the grave as prophesied, He was raised to sit on the throne of David at the right hand of God. Peter quotes Psalm 110:1 and forcefully applies it to Jesus. Truly it could apply to no other.

Conclusion

We have looked at fifty-six different prophecies that comprised a remarkably detailed picture of the Promised Messiah. It is important to realize that the fifty-six we examined are but a portion of the total number. Each one of them was fulfilled completely and exactly. Where faith was before, it can only be strengthened. Where it was not, perhaps this study will motivate to further investigation.

When God promises something, it takes place. This has been demonstrated fifty-six times. In closing, I want to notice one other promise, a promise yet to be fulfilled. It is found in the 14th chapter of John, verses 1-3. There Jesus says:

Do not let your heart be troubled; believe in God, believe also in Me. In My Father's house are many dwelling places; if it were not so, I would have told you; for I go to prepare a place for you. If I go and prepare a place for you, I will come again and receive you to Myself, that where I am, there you may be also.

"Come, Lord Jesus" (Rev. 22:20).

Bibliography

Barclay, William. *The Gospel of Matthew,* "The Daily Bible Study Series." Philadelphia: Westminster Press, 1976.

Barnes, Albert. *Barnes Notes on the New Testament.* Grand Rapids: Kregel Publications, 1962.

Baxter, J. S. *Explore the Book.* Grand Rapids: Zondervan Publications, 1966.

Beck, William F. *What Does* Almah *Mean?* The Lutheran News, 1967.

Cooper, David L. *God and Messiah.* Los Angeles: Biblical Research Society.

Davis, John D. *Davis' Dictionary of the Bible,* Fourth Revised Edition. Grand Rapids: Baker House, 1977.

Farrar, Frederick. *The Life of Christ.* Dutton, Dovar: Cassell & Co., 1897.

Fausett, A. R. *A Commentary Critical, Experimental and Practical on the Old and New Testaments.* Grand Rapids: Wm. B. Eerdman Publishing Co., 1961.

Hailey, Homer. *A Commentary on the Minor Prophets.* Grand Rapids: Baker Book House, 1972.

Hailey, Homer. *From Creation to the Day of Eternity.* Las Vegas: Nevada Publications, 1973.

Hailey, Homer. *That You May Believe – Studies in the Gospel of John.* Las Vegas: Nevada Publications, 1973.

Hengstenberg, E. W. *Christology of the Old Testament.* Grand Rapids: Kregel Publications, 1970.

Henry, Matthew. *Matthew Henry's Commentary in One Volume.* Wilmington: Sovereign Grace Publishers, 1972.

Hovey, Alvah. *An American Commentary on the New Testament – Matthew.* Philadelphia: American Baptist Publications Society, 1886.

Jamieson, Robert, A.R. Fausset and David Brown. *Commentary on the Whole Bible.* Grand Rapids: Zondervan Publishing House, 1961.

Macknight, James. *Apostolic Epistles.* Nashville: Gospel Advocate Co., 1960

Magath, Julius. *Jesus Before the Sanhedrin.* Nashville: Southern Methodist Publishing House, 1886.

McCord, Hugo. *Messianic Prophecy.* Nashville: 20th Century Christian, 1976.

McDowell, Josh. *Evidence That Demands a Verdict.* Campus Crusade for Christ, 1972.

McGarvey, J.W. *New Commentary on Acts of Apostles.* Cincinnati: Standard Publishing Co., 1892

McGarvey, J.W. and Pendleton, Philip Y. *The Fourfold Gospel.* Cincinnati: Standard Publishing Co., 1914.

Orr, James and others, eds. *The International Standard Bible Encyclopedia.* Grand Rapids: Wm. B. Eerdman Publishing Co., 1976

Spence, H. D. M. and Exell, Joseph S. *The Pulpit Commentary.* Grand Rapids: Wm. B. Eerdman Publishing Co., 1950.

Spurgeon, C. H. *The Treasury of David.* Grand Rapids: Baker Book House, 1978.

Vine, W. E. *Expository Dictionary of New Testament Words.* Old Tappan: Fleming H. Revell Co., 1940.

Wallace, Foy E. Jr. *God's Prophetic Word.* Ft. Worth: Foy E. Wallace, Jr. Publications, 1946.

Woods, Guy N. *The Living Messages of the Books of the Old Testament.* Spiritual Sword Lectureship. Jonesboro (AR): National Christian Press, Inc., 1977.